SHAKESPEARE'S ALTERNATIVE TALES

LONGMAN MEDIEVAL AND RENAISSANCE LIBRARY

General Editors:
CHARLOTTE BREWER, Hertford College, Oxford
N.H. KEEBLE, University of Stirling

Published Titles:

Leah Scragg

Shakespeare's Alternative Tales

LONGMAN
LONDON AND NEW YORK

Addison Wesley Longman Limited
Edinburgh Gate
Harlow, Essex CM20 2JE, England
and Associated Companies throughout the world.

*Published in the United States of America
by Addison Wesley Longman Publishing, New York*

© Addison Wesley Longman Limited 1996

First Published 1996

ISBN 0 582 244854 CSD
ISBN 0 582 244846 PPR

British Library Cataloging-in-Publication Data
A catalogue record for this book is available from the British Library

Library of Congress Cataloguing-in-Publication Data
A catalogue record for this book has been applied for.

Set by 8 in 10/12pt Bembo
Produced by Longman Singapore Publishers (Pte) Ltd.
Printed in Singapore

Like an old tale still

(*The Winter's Tale*, V.ii.62)

Contents

Acknowledgements

The New Arden editions of Shakespeare's plays are quoted throughout, and I would like to thank the publishers, Routledge, for their kind permission to use them. I am also heavily indebted to Geoffrey Bullough (1957–75) *Narrative and Dramatic Sources of Shakespeare*, and am grateful, once again, to Routledge for their permission to quote several passages at length. On a more personal level I would like to thank Neil Keeble for all his advice and assistance in the course of both this and my previous book, and Julia Briggs for a generous exchange of ideas on the theme of the substitute bedmate that provided the starting point for Chapter 6. I would also like to take this opportunity to add my mite to the debt of gratitude owed by all students of Shakespeare's sources to Geoffrey Bullough's work.

Introduction

> Now therein of all sciences (I speak still of human, and according to the human conceits) is our poet the monarch. For he doth not only show the way, but giveth so sweet a prospect into the way, as will entice any man to enter into it. Nay, he doth, as if your journey should lie through a fair vineyard, at the first give you a cluster of grapes, that full of that taste, you may long to pass further. He beginneth not with obscure definitions, which must blur the margent with interpretations, and load the memory with doubtfulness; but he cometh to you with words set in delightful proportion, either accompanied with, or prepared for, the well enchanting skill of music; and with a tale forsooth he cometh unto you, with a tale which holdeth children from play, and old men from the chimney corner.
>
> (Sir Philip Sidney, *An Apology for Poetry*, pub.1595)[1]

The educational value of tales, and hence the importance of the literary forms through which they are transmitted, is central to Renaissance literary theory and constitutes a major weapon in the armoury of those writers seeking to uphold the importance of the arts. Sidney's encomium, quoted above, is typical of the stance adopted by literary apologists of the period, while the value of stories as a vehicle for moral instruction is endorsed by a range of practising writers engaged with works of a variety of kinds. Sir Thomas Elyot in *The Boke Named the Governour* (1531), for example, inserts the tale of Titus and Gisippus into the middle of a political treatise, justifying his procedure on the grounds of the model of conduct and mental refreshment that it offers the reader, cf:

> But now in the midst of my labour, as it were to pause and take breath, and also to recreate the readers, which, fatigued with long precepts, desire variety of matter, or some new pleasant fable or history, I will rehearse a right goodly

---

1. Quoted from Geoffrey Shepherd (ed.) (1973) *An Apology for Poetry*, University Press, Manchester, p.113. Though not published until 1595, Sidney's work was composed during the period 1581–3 and circulated in manuscript prior to publication.

example of friendship. Which example, studiously read, shall minister to the readers singular pleasure and also incredible comfort to practise amity.[2]

Edmund Spenser, in his epic poem *The Faerie Queene* (1590 and 1596), similarly employs a chivalric fiction as a vehicle for the inculcation of the Christian virtues, defending its use, in the letter to Sir Walter Raleigh that constitutes the introduction to the poem, on the basis of the efficacy of such stories in capturing the attention of the reader:

> The general end therefore of all the book is to fashion a gentleman or noble person in virtuous and gentle discipline, which for that I conceived should be most plausible and pleasing, being coloured with an historical fiction, the which the most part of men delight to read, rather for variety of matter than for profit of the example, I chose the history of King Arthur, as most fit for the excellency of his person, being made famous by many men's former works.[3]

As Spenser's closing sentence suggests, the stories to which Renaissance writers turned to secure the attention of their audiences were not original compositions, but were drawn in the main from a substantial literary stock, itself a hybrid of classical material, mediaeval romance and Italian novella. Tales were valued not for their novelty, but their antiquity,[4] and had frequently undergone a long process of adaptation in the course of their history, becoming encrusted with meanings in the process of their evolution. For Sir Thomas Elyot the story of Titus and Gisippus, while being an entertaining collection of incidents, is also 'the description of friendship engendered by the similitude of age and personage, augmented by the conformity of manners and studies',[5] while for Spenser Arthur is the 'image of a brave knight', and may thus be presented as 'perfected in the twelve private moral virtues'.[6] In retelling a particular story a Renaissance writer was consequently engaged, not

---

2. Quotation based on the text in Geoffrey Bullough (1957–75) *Narrative and Dramatic Sources of Shakespeare*, vol. i, Routledge and Kegan Paul, p. 212. Spelling and punctuation, however, have been modernized.

3. Quotation based on J.C. Smith and E. de Selincourt (eds) (1912) *The Poetical Works of Edmund Spenser*, Oxford University Press, p. 407. Spelling and punctuation, however, have been modernized.

4. See the opening lines of Shakespeare's *Pericles* in which the narrator (the mediaeval poet, Gower) stresses the long history, and beneficial effects, of the story he is about to present (cf. 'It has been sung at festivals, / On ember-eves and holy-ales; / And lords and ladies in their lives / Have read it for restoratives', 1 Chorus, 5–8).

5. From Bullough, *Narrative and Dramatic Sources of Shakespeare*, vol.i, p. 217. Spelling has been modernized.

6. From Smith and de Selincourt (eds) *The Poetical Works of Edmund Spenser*, p. 407. Spelling has been modernized.

simply in reshaping the structure of a particular narrative, or recasting it in a more modern idiom, but in participating in a species of debate with earlier writers and the meanings that their tales had accrued. The choice of a particular story was governed, not solely by the interest of the narrative, but the system of ideas to which it referred, ideas with which, in the case of many items, even the least educated members of a Renaissance audience would be familiar (cf. the parables of Christ). Shakespeare, in common with his contemporaries, drew heavily on this literary stock, and the stories on which his plays are constructed, like the tales employed by Elyot and Spenser, did not descend to him as innocent collections of incidents, but brought with them considerable cultural baggage, substantially lost to the modern reader, but an essential component for the contemporary spectator of the experience of the plays.

It is the dialogue in which Shakespeare engages with the conventional meanings of the tales on which he draws that is the subject of this book. Whereas the companion volume, *Shakespeare's Mouldy Tales*, locates the dramatist's approach to his source materials within the context of Renaissance attitudes to adaptation, tracing the history of a number of inherited plot motifs in their progress through the corpus, the present study focuses on a smaller group of plays in which the playwright's treatment of his source materials, and hence the meanings associated with them, is rather more radical than the term 'adaptation' suggests. The plays considered here, drawn from a variety of genres and different periods of Shakespeare's career, are those in which the expectations generated by a familiar story are in some way overthrown: the moral of the action is not the conventional one, characters fail to behave in accordance with audience expectation, or function in a mirror-image version of a traditional structure. Rather than realizing new potentialities within a conventional framework, expanding the significance of a familiar complex of motifs, the plays interrogate the assumptions implicit in their inherited materials, creating an interplay for a contemporary audience between 'received' and 'alternative' readings of a text. Consequently, whereas *Shakespeare's Mouldy Tales* seeks to position Shakespearian drama against sixteenth-century attitudes to the creative process, this book is concerned with the history of the tales that the dramatist employs, with the tissue of meanings that surrounds them, and the cultural tensions that are exhibited through the playwright's departures from expected stances or patterns of event.

The scrutiny to which contemporary ideologies are subjected in a number of these plays, through their heterodox treatment of inherited materials, gives them a particular interest for contemporary criticism with its emphasis upon cultural issues and the text as a product of historical and social processes. The treatment of the tale of the prodigal son, for example, in *1 Henry IV* lends itself to discussion in terms of New Historicist theories of subversion and containment, while the emphasis on female experience in Shakespeare's version of the chivalric quest in *All's Well That Ends Well* is of obvious interest to Feminist criticism. At the same time, the radical nature of Shakespeare's departures from his inherited stories in these plays affords the modern reader with relatively little knowledge of contemporary literary theory a number of clear illustrations of the process of interrogation at work in the corpus, and thus a comparatively straightforward means of introduction to some recent critical developments and their application to the Shakespearian canon. The failure of the characters of *Measure for Measure* to conform to the expectations generated by the tale of the heroic sacrifice, for example, highlights that resistance to a dominant ideology which is the focus of Cultural Materialism, while the unconventionally positive role played by a bastard son in *The Life and Death of King John* serves as a pointer to a wider process of 'legitimation' of central interest to New Historicist critics. The tales that are explored here are thus 'alternative' in more than one sense. On the one hand, they involve the radical reworking of familiar motifs, while on the other they are susceptible to analysis in terms of new and contentious methodologies at variance with traditional critical procedures.

While the subject matter of this study seeks to illustrate the validity of Sidney's dictum with regard to the potency of tales and their enduring value as instruments for the exploration and promulgation of ideas, the procedures employed in the course of it are designed to emulate his strategy for sustaining the reader's interest. Rather than beginning 'with obscure definitions, which must blur the margent with interpretations, and load the memory with doubtfulness', each chapter begins with a tale which has traditionally held 'children from play, and old men from the chimney corner', its history and the ideological assumptions upon which it is founded supplying a context for the investigation of a specific Shakespearian play. The dramatist's heterodox treatment of his inherited story in turn forms an introduction to one or more recent critical approaches to the text, affording the reader a means of access to some new ways of engaging with the work. The overall aim of the study is thus to encourage the student or general reader to 'long to pass further' into a number of fields. The contextualization of the plays is designed to exhibit the continuing interest and importance of the investigation of Shakespeare's sources, while the exploration of the process of adaptation in which the dramatist engages may be seen as an introduction to the dialogic nature of Renaissance drama as a whole. Above all, however, it is hoped that the book will assist those daunted by the 'obscure definitions' of modern literary theory to come to grips with some late twentieth-century ways of approaching the Shakespearian corpus, and thus will 'entice' them towards a deeper investigation of the many new meanings currently being elicited by contemporary writers from the old tale of the dramatist's work.

Chapter 1

1 *Henry IV* and the Tale of the Prodigal Son

A certain man had two sons.

And the younger of them said to his father, Father, give me the portion of the goods that falleth to me. So he divided unto them his substance.

So not long after when the younger son had gathered all together, he took his journey into a far country, and there he wasted his goods with riotous living.

Now when he had spent all, there arose a great dearth throughout that land, and he began to be in necessity.

Then he went and clave to a citizen of that country and he sent him to his farm to feed swine.

And he would fain have filled his belly with the husks that the swine ate: but no man gave them him.

Then he came to himself, and said, How many hired servants at my fathers have bread enough, and I die for hunger.

I will rise and go to my father, and say unto him, Father, I have sinned against heaven, and before thee,

And am no more worthy to be called thy son: make me as one of thy hired servants.

So he arose, and came to his father, and when he was yet a great way off, his father saw him, and had compassion, and ran and fell on his neck, and kissed him.

And the son said unto him, Father, I have sinned against heaven, and before thee, and am no more worthy to be called thy son.

Then the father said to his servants, Bring forth the best robe, and put it on him, and put a ring on his hand, and shoes on his feet,

And bring the fat calf, and kill him, and let us
eat and be merry.

For this my son was dead, and is alive again: and he
was lost, but he is found. And they began to be merry.

Now the elder brother was in the field, and when he
came and drew near to the house, he heard melody and dancing,

And called one of his servants, and asked what these
things meant.

And he said unto him, Thy brother is come and thy father
hath killed the fatted calf, because he hath received
him safe and sound.

Then he was angry, and would not go in: therefore came
his father out and entreated him.

But he answered and said to his father, Lo, these many
years have I done thee service, and neither brake I at
any time thy commandment, yet thou never gavest me a kid,
that I might make merry with my friends.

But when this thy son was come, which hath devoured
thy goods with harlots, thou hast for his sake killed
the fatted calf.

And he said unto him, Son, thou art ever with me, and
all that I have is thine. It is meet that we should
make merry, and be glad: for this thy brother was dead,
and is alive again: and he was lost, but he is found.

(*St. Luke*, 15:11–31)

The tale of the prodigal son, quoted here from the Geneva Bible with
which Shakespeare would have been familiar,[1] was among the parables
most popular with Renaissance schoolmasters, and most frequently performed on the Tudor stage. The story, as the marginal commentary in
sixteenth-century editions of the Bible explained, taught that man should
not separate himself from his heavenly father, that God is ever ready to
accept the repentant sinner, and that no-one should begrudge the mercy
shown to the penitent soul. Nevertheless, though essentially concerned
with the relationship between the Christian deity and the human race, the
parable acquired in the course of its history a somewhat different application. Since the central character is a young man whose misguided actions

---

1. See Naseeb Shaheen (1989) *Biblical References in Shakespeare's Plays*, Associated
University Presses, pp. 20–5 and 149–50. All subsequent biblical quotations are from
the Geneva edition, but spelling and punctuation (as in the passage quoted above) have
been modernized.

bring about his undoing, the tale naturally lent itself to the instruction of the young and thus to the educational aims of humanist scholars. Prodigal Son plays devised by English and continental schoolmasters date from early in the century, and the lessons that they inculcate do not always coincide with those of the story told by Christ. Some plays, like the neo-Latin *Acolastus*, a highly influential play by Willem de Volder translated into English by John Palsgrave in 1540, merely elaborate upon the Biblical parable, developing the theme of man's profligacy and stressing the availability of grace. Others enforce much harsher lessons – the need to enforce parental discipline, the danger of spoiling children, and the misery of mind and body that attends the sinful life. The surviving fragment of an interlude (*Pater, Filius et Uxor*) printed in England c.1530 is indicative of this development. The son is already in a state of poverty when the play opens, and is engaged in selling faggots at the behest of a shrewish wife. In this instance, though the father is grieved at his son's condition, he is unable to come to his aid, and the younger man's repentance is therefore unavailing. The growing secularization of the story implicit in the moral of this episode is seen even more plainly in Thomas Ingelend's *The Disobedient Child* (c.1559–70). Here the father attempts to persuade the son of the value of study, but his advice to apply himself to work is spurned by the younger man who insists upon taking a wife, and then in living beyond his means. The couple are reduced to penury and the son seeks the father's help, only to be told that as a married man he is beyond his father's assistance. In this case, not only does the emphasis fall upon the worldly punishment of the sinner, but the figure who once represented the heavenly father has himself become a target for criticism in that he over-indulges his son in his formative years.

The distance travelled during the century by the Biblical story (which is bound up with the religious developments that take place in the course of this period, notably the spread of Protestantism) is indicated by the Prologue to the anonymous anti-Catholic moral interlude *Nice Wanton* (1547–53). Though the play follows the inherited pattern of indulgent parent, virtuous and corrupt offspring, repentance (in the case of the daughter), and the hope of eternal life, the erring parent is now a mother, while the lesson that the play teaches is not God's readiness to extend his forgiveness but the importance of education, and the need to exert proper authority in the home, cf:

> The prudent Prince Solomon doth say,
> He that spareth the rod, the child doth hate,
> He would youth should be kept in awe alway

By correction in time at reasonable rate:
To be taught to fear God, and their parents obey,
To get learning and qualities, thereby to maintain
An honest quiet life, correspondent alway
To God's law and the king's, for it is certain,
If children be noseled in idleness and ill,
And brought up therein, it is hard to restrain,
And draw them from natural wont evil,
As here in this interlude ye shall see plain.[2]

The sequence of events enacted by the Prodigal Son dramas had much in common with the structure of the Morality plays produced during the same period, and in time a considerable overlap took place between the two. The Morality play enacts an allegorical battle between good and evil for the soul of man, with a representative human figure initially dedicating himself to virtue, corrupted by a group of vices, brought to penury and thence to repentance. Like the Prodigal Son play, the form was appropriated during the first half of the sixteenth century by those concerned with the education of the young, with a number of plays (e.g. Wever's *Lusty Juventus*, 1547–53) specifically directed towards a youthful audience. Since the vices – wenching, dicing, drinking – to which youth falls subject are common to both kinds of play, figures found their way from one genre to the other, producing a blend between literal and allegorical modes. In *Nice Wanton*, for example, the fall of the misguided daughter, Dalilah, is signalled by her acquaintance with a character named Iniquity, while the central figure of Palsgrave's version of *Acolastus* is given the alternative, explanatory, name of 'Stroygood'.

The dominant dramatic form of the sixteenth century, the History play, exhibits in turn the influence of the hybrid Prodigal Son/Morality type. Until very late in the century the majority of Histories followed a common pattern, beginning with a monarch (often a young man) in a position of security, showing his descent into depravity through corrupt advice, and tracing the consequent dereliction of his kingdom, until a return to wise government restores both king and realm to their former state. The rich man's son of the Prodigal Son plays, or Rex Humanitas of the Moralities thus acquires a specific name, while the kingdom that he loses is not a heavenly one but an earthly place. Robert Greene's *James IV* (c.1590–1) is typical of the genre. The play opens with the marriage between the young James IV of Scotland and the daughter of

---

2. Quoted from W. Carew Hazlitt (ed.) (1874) *A Select Collection of Old English Plays, Originally published by Robert Dodsley*, vol. ii, 4th edn, Reeves and Turner, p. 163.

the English king, and thus at a moment of both personal fulfilment and political stability. The young king falls prey, however, to the vicious counsels of the evil Ateukin who encourages him to yield to his lust for another woman, and to seek the life of his virtuous queen. The corruption at the heart of public life feeds down into the lower social orders, and the weakened kingdom is unable to resist an English invasion. James repents, however, of his errors, is forgiven by the queen and her avenging father, and the corrupt counsellor is punished. The anonymous *Thomas of Woodstock* (1591–5), tracing the career of the young Richard II, follows a similar pattern. The young king again gives ear to the advice of flatterers, squanders his substance on youthful follies, and seeks the lives of the uncles who endeavour to restrain him by their counsels. The conclusion of the drama is no longer extant, but the flatterers are killed in the civil war that occurs before the play breaks off, and the young king sees their deaths as a punishment for his sins.

The similarities between the Histories and the hybrid Prodigal Son/Moralities led, not unnaturally, to the transfer of characters and devices from plays overtly concerned with man's spiritual condition to dramas ostensibly dealing with worldly affairs. In Bale's *King Johan* (1538–60), for example, many of the characters have both literal and allegorical names. Stephen Langton, thus appears as Sedition, the Pope is Usurped Power, and Simon of Swinsett is Dissimulation. King Johan (John), a historical figure, engages in conversation with a character representing England, while Veritas explains the significance of the play's events to the audience. Similarly, Greene's *James IV* includes a debate between representative figures, a lawyer, a merchant and a divine, while the extraordinarily corrupt actions of the monarch are brushed aside non-naturalistically as the understandable failings of youth (cf. V.vi.160) in order to complete the familiar process of fall, repentance and reclamation.

The career of Prince Hal (1387–1422), who succeeded to the throne as Henry V, particularly lent itself to treatment in accordance with this didactic pattern in that art and life, in his case, were thought to coincide. Tales of the wildness of the Prince's youth and of his abrupt conversion to the ideal monarch on his accession to the throne date from early in the fifteenth century, and were current in his own lifetime. As early as c.1421, at least a year before the King's death, Thomas Walsingham noted that the Prince became a changed man on succeeding his father,[3] while Tito Livio in his semi-official *Vita Henrici Quinti*

3. See V.H. Galbraith (ed.) (1937) *The St Albans Chronicle, 1406–1420*, Clarendon Press, p. 69.

(c.1437), records the licence of Hal's early years.[4] The tradition continued, moreover, into the sixteenth century. Robert Fabyan's *Chronicle* (pub. 1516) describes the young Prince as being given to 'all vyce and insolency' prior to his accession, and as a 'newe man' after his father's death,[5] while later chroniclers stress the wildness of his early career. Sir Thomas Elyot, for example, records in *The Boke Named the Governour* (1531) that he was imprisoned for resisting the power of the Lord Chief Justice;[6] John Stowe notes in his *Chronicles* (1580), that he took part in highway robberies;[7] while Raphael Holinshed (who attributes many of the stories surrounding the Prince to malicious gossip) relates that he took the crown from his father's pillow (*Chronicles*, 1587).[8] Not unnaturally, the story of the ungoverned prince who repents of his errors and becomes a model king found its way from historical works into the drama of the period, and the earliest extant treatment of Hal's career is clearly influenced by the hybrid Prodigal Son/Morality tradition. *The Famous Victories of Henry V* (Anon, 1583–8) presents the young prince as a highly dissolute young man, contemptuous of his father's authority, and anxious for his death. The play opens with him counting the spoils of a robbery and tyrannizing over his father's officials, while his frequent oaths and and threats of violence testify to the depravity of his nature. The first scene concludes with his assertion that, were the King dead, he and his corrupt companions would rule the realm in their own way, a theme reiterated throughout the early part of the play:

> All.   We are ready to wait upon your Grace.
> Hen 5.   Gogs wounds! Wait? We will go all together.
>   We are all fellows. I tell you, sirs, and the King
>   My father were dead, we would all be kings.
>   Therefore come away.
>
> (Scene i, lines 91–5)[9]

4. See C.L. Kingsford (ed.) (1911) *The First English Life of Henry the Fifth* (1513), Clarendon Press.
5. Quoted from A.R. Humphreys (ed.) (1960) *The First Part of King Henry IV*, The Arden Shakespeare, Methuen, p. xxix.
6. See Geoffrey Bullough (1957–75), *Narrative and Dramatic Sources of Shakespeare*, vol. iv, Routledge and Kegan Paul, pp. 288–9.
7. See Bullough, *Narrative and Dramatic Sources of Shakespeare*, vol. iv, p. 219.
8. See Richard Hosley (ed.) (1968) *An Edition of Holinshed's Chronicles (1587)*, G.P. Putnam's Sons, p. 116.
9. All quotations from *The Famous Victories of Henry V* are based upon the edition in Bullough, *Narrative and Dramatic Sources of Shakespeare*, vol. iv, pp. 299–343. Spelling and punctuation, however, have been modernized.

Compare:

> Hen 5. Here's such ado nowadays. Here's 'prisoning, here's
> hanging, whipping, and the devil and all: but I tell you,
> sirs, when I am King we will have no such thing, but my lads,
> if the old King my father were dead, we would all be kings.
> Joh. Old[castle]. He is a good old man. God take him
> to his mercy the sooner.
> Hen 5. But, Ned, so soon as I am King, the first
> thing I will do shall be to put my Lord Chief Justice
> out of office. And thou shalt be my Lord Chief Justice
> of England.
> Ned. Shall I be Lord Chief Justice?
> By Gog's wounds, I'll be the bravest Lord Chief Justice
> that ever was in England.
> Hen 5. Then, Ned, I'll turn all these
> prisons into fence schools, and will endue thee with
> them, with lands to maintain them withall. Then I will
> have a bout with my Lord Chief Justice. Thou shalt hang
> none but pick-purses and horse stealers, and such base-
> minded fellows. But that fellow that will stand by the
> highway side courageously with his sword and buckler and
> take a purse, that fellow give him commendations. Beside
> that, send him to me, and I will give him an annual pension
> out of my exchequer to maintain him all the days of his life.
> Joh. Nobly spoken, Harry, we shall
> never have a merry world till the old king be dead.

(Scene vi, lines 453–76)

The anarchic attitudes displayed here are not merely a matter of idle words. In the course of the drama the Prince takes part in a riot (cf. Scene ii, 192ff.), assaults the Lord Chief Justice (Scene iv, line 357), and waits upon his dying father in a cloak full of needles signifying that he 'stand[s] upon thorns' (Scene vi, line 487) until the crown is on his head. The King's attitude to his ungracious offspring confirms, more-over, the didactic tradition to which the drama belongs. While the son's eagerness to possess his patrimony echoes the Prodigal Son's desire for the premature enjoyment of his father's wealth, the King's grief at the degenerate nature of his son recalls the regret for parental failure expressed by the sorrowing fathers of earlier plays, cf:

> Hen. 4. And is it true, my Lord, that my son is
> already sent to the Fleet? Now, truly, that
> man [i.e. the Lord Chief Justice] is fitter to rule the realm

than I, for by no means could I rule my son, and he by one
word hath caused him to be ruled. Oh, my son, my son, no sooner
out of one prison but into another. I had thought once,
whiles I had lived, to have seen this noble realm of
England flourish by thee my son, but now I see it goes
to ruin and decay.

(Scene vi, lines 509–16)

It is the encounter between the Prince and his father, and the
former's conversion from his corrupt life, that demonstrates most
plainly, however, the overlap between the history play and the Prodigal
Son tradition. Harry enters his father's presence in a wholly degenerate
state, determined to 'clap the crown on [his] head' (Scene vi, lines
480–1) as soon as the breath is out of the King's mouth, and contemptuous of the suggestion that he might reform (cf. Scene vi, lines
491–4). No sooner is he greeted, however, by his weeping father, than he
instantly repents, the terms in which he does so locating his conduct
within a spiritual rather than a political arena. The King laments that his
son has left him for 'vile and reprobate company, which abuseth youth so
manifestly' (Scene vi, lines 543–4), upon which the 'conscience' (line
553) of the younger man is stirred. Consigning his cloak of needles to the
devil, the 'master of all mischief' (line 568), he laments, like his Biblical
predecessor, that he is unworthy of the position he might once have
claimed (line 564), and resolves to withdraw into 'some solitary place' to
'lament [his] sinful life' (lines 571–2). His repentance, moreover, as in the
parable, effects an instantaneous reconciliation with his father. Not only
does the King pardon him, but he invokes upon him the blessing of God,
thus readmitting him both to his former place within the family and kingdom and to the ranks of the spiritually redeemed (lines 577–9).

The complex of dramatic works enacting the fall and redemption/
damnation of misguided youth remained popular throughout the sixteenth century and continued to be played long after the emergence of
the first major dramatists of the Elizabethan-Jacobean era. Histories and
Moralities appear on the English stage throughout the Tudor period,
while English actors performed Prodigal Son plays on the continent well
into the seventeenth century.[10] In taking up the story of Prince Hal in *1
Henry IV* (c.1596-7) Shakespeare was thus operating against the background of a long-familiar dramatic tradition, generating specific

---

10. See Alfred Harbage, revised by S. Schoenbaum (1964) *The Annals of English Drama
975–1700*, Methuen, pp. 206–7.

audience expectations and governed by an established set of conventions. These conventions, moreover, were overtly homiletic. The story of the princely prodigal with its four traditional elements – indulgent father, dutiful and undutiful offspring, enlightenment and repentance – was a profoundly moral one, inculcating the necessity of repentance, the merciful nature of the deity and the inexorable relationship between right conduct and worldly/spiritual success. That Shakespeare was aware of the monitory nature of this tradition is confirmed by his own contribution to its development. *Richard II* (1594–5), the first play in the tetralogy to which *1 Henry IV* belongs, follows the career of a youthful monarch who, like the young kings of *Thomas of Woodstock* or *James IV*, falls away from the standard of conduct expected of a prince, gives ear to the advice of flatterers, squanders his royal patrimony and ultimately faces the loss of his crown. The career of Richard hangs over *1 Henry IV* and the terms in which he is mentioned clearly align him with the feckless youths of the prodigal tradition. In III.ii, for example, Henry IV warns Hal of the dangers of failing to sustain the dignity of his rank by citing the similarity between his behaviour and that of the previous monarch:

> The skipping King, he ambled up and down,
> With shallow jesters, and rash bavin wits,
> Soon kindled and soon burnt, carded his state,
> Mingled his royalty with cap'ring fools,
> Had his great name profaned with their scorns,
> And gave his countenance against his name
> To laugh at gibing boys, and stand the push
> Of every beardless vain comparative,
> Grew a companion to the common streets,
> Enfeoff'd himself to popularity.
> ...
> So, when he had occasion to be seen,
> He was but as the cuckoo is in June,
> Heard, not regarded.
>
> (III.ii.60–76)

The sources on which Shakespeare drew in constructing the story of his second royal spendthrift invited a similarly paradigmatic treatment. Though his political material is mainly derived from Holinshed, who (as noted above) largely exculpates the Prince, the scenes dealing with Hal's waywardness clearly look back to *The Famous Victories of Henry V* in which the conventional wildness-repentance-success sequence is vividly re-enacted. The opening scenes of *1 Henry IV*, moreover, encourage the spectator to suppose that the action of the play will correspond to that of the traditional story. The drama opens with the King's announcement that he intends to participate in a crusade, the objective immediately locating the action within a Christian framework, and encouraging those outside the play world to view Henry's court in a favourable light. A clear contrast is then set up between the Duke of Northumberland's worthy son and the King's degenerate offspring, evoking the traditional opposition between provident and prodigal youths. On being told of Hotspur's heroic conduct on the battlefield, for example, the King laments the very different behaviour of the heir to the throne:

> There thou mak'st me sad, and mak'st me sin
> In envy that my Lord Northumberland
> Should be the father to so blest a son;
> A son who is the theme of honour's tongue,
> Amongst a grove the very straightest plant,
> Who is sweet Fortune's minion and her pride;
> Whilst I by looking on the praise of him
> See riot and dishonour stain the brow
> Of my young Harry. O that it could be prov'd
> That some night-tripping fairy had exchang'd
> In cradle clothes our children where they lay,
> And call'd mine Percy, his Plantagenet!
>
> (I.i.77–88)

Once again, the lexis employed here serves to widen the play's action from the temporal to the spiritual arena: the King 'sin[s]' in envying Northumberland who is 'blest' in the possession of a worthy son. As in the Tudor Morality play Hotspur's dutifulness is expressed by right conduct ('Amongst a grove the very straightest plant') and yields success in the wordly sphere ('sweet fortune's minion'), while Hal's gracelessness is defined by 'riot' and is productive of 'dishonour'.

The majority of I.ii in which the Prince himself first appears reinforces the expectations generated by dramatic precedent and evoked by the play's opening lines. The scene is set in a tavern, the conventional location for the seduction of the young, and the exchanges between Hal and Falstaff are rich in references to the vices – drinking (I.ii.2), feasting (I.ii.3), wenching (I.ii.8–10), stealing (I.ii.13–15) – to which misguided youth invariably falls subject. The figure of Falstaff, with his huge belly, indifference to time, and addiction to the pleasures of the flesh, is the embodiment of physical indulgence and spiritual neglect, and a number of references both in this and later scenes serve to equate him with those traditional agents of man's corruption – the world, the flesh and the devil. Poins declares in I.ii that he sold his soul to the devil 'for a cup of Madeira and a cold capon's leg' (110–13); the Prince (impersonating his father) refers to him as 'that reverend vice, that grey iniquity' (II.iv.447–8), and as a 'villainous abominable misleader of youth' an 'old white-bearded Satan' (II.iv.456–7); while Falstaff declares that were Hal to banish him he would be exiling himself from 'the world' (II.iv.474). At the same time, his energy, delight in mischief, and verbal facility align him with the vice of the hybrid Prodigal Son/Morality tradition (cf. 'thou reverend vice' II.iv.447), inviting the audience to view him as the King's antagonist in a contest for Hal's allegiance.

The concept of Falstaff as an alternative, corrupt, father figure, leading impressionable youth from the path of virtue, is acted out in II.iv. Hal and Falstaff rehearse a forthcoming interview between the Prince and his father with Falstaff playing the part of the King, complete with a mockery throne and a cushion for a crown. In the anarchic universe thus created, vice and virtue become reversed, and Falstaff is able to advance a favourable self-image designed to endear him to his listeners:

> Fal. There is a thing, Harry, which thou
>   hast often heard of, and it is known to many in our land
>   by the name of pitch. This pitch (as ancient writers do report)
>   doth defile, so doth the company thou keepest ... And yet
>   there is a virtuous man whom I have often noted in thy company,
>   but I know not his name.
> Prince. What manner of man, and it like your Majesty?
> Fal. A goodly portly man, i'faith, and a corpulent;
>   of a cheerful look, a pleasing eye, and a most noble carriage;
>   and, as I think, his age some fifty, or by'r lady inclining to
>   threescore; and now I remember me, his name is Falstaff. If
>   that man be lewdly given, he deceiveth me; for, Harry, I see
>   virtue in his looks. If then the tree may be known by the fruit,
>   as the fruit by the tree, then peremptorily I speak it, there
>   is virtue in that Falstaff; him keep with, the rest banish.
>
> (II.iv.406–25)

The field of reference employed here is characteristic of Falstaff. His language is rich in scriptural allusions, a fact of which a contemporary audience would have been keenly aware, and his frequent recourse to Biblical words and phrases functions to sustain on the part of the spectator a constant awareness of the world view to which his own life stands opposed. In this passage the reference to pitch is derived from *Ecclesiasticus*, 13.1, while the tree being known by its fruit is a familiar New Testament text (*Luke*, 6.44). Two of these recurrent allusions are of particular interest here in that they are drawn from the parable of the Prodigal Son. In III.iii, Falstaff, quarrelling with the Hostess of the Boar's Head over the reckoning and claiming that his pocket has been picked, asks in assumed anger whether she will 'make a yonker' out of him (77–8). The term 'yonker' (i.e. younger son) was frequently employed as an alternative for 'prodigal', Falstaff's accusation against the Hostess looking back to the hybrid Prodigal Son/Morality plays in which erring youth was exploited and frequently robbed in a tavern. The second reference is more explicit. In IV.ii Falstaff soliloquizes on the miserable condition of the troops he has pressed into service reflecting that, were he to be met with them, he would be thought to have fallen into the company of 'a hundred and fifty tattered prodigals lately come from swine-keeping, from eating draff and husks' (34–5). Not only does the reference confirm Shakespeare's awareness of the parable in the course of composing the play, it also contributes to the association the drama establishes between Falstaff and the corruption of youth.

While the first two acts of the drama locate the prince within the context of the prodigal tradition, the last three, superficially at least, act out the conventional process of repentance and reacceptance. The Prince appears before his father in III.ii and the terms in which the King greets him sustain the spiritual dimension of the action. Henry wonders whether the Prince's wildness is a punishment for his own sins, emphasizing the social depths to which he has sunk:

> I know not whether God will have it so
> For some displeasing service I have done,
> That in his secret doom out of my blood
> He'll breed revengement and a scourge for me;
> But thou dost in thy passages of life
> Make me believe that thou art only mark'd
> For the hot vengeance and the rod of heaven,
> To punish my mistreadings. Tell me else
> Could such inordinate and low desires,
> Such poor, such bare, such lewd, such mean attempts,
> Such barren pleasures, rude society,

As thou art match'd withal, and grafted to,
Accompany the greatness of thy blood,
And hold their level with thy princely heart?

(III.ii.4–17)

While the Prince attributes many of the stories regarding him to slanderous gossip, he nevertheless admits to his 'irregular' (27) conduct, seeking 'pardon' through 'true submission' (28), and promising to wash away his shame in the blood of their enemies, and thus to regain, through virtuous action, his rightful place as his father's son:

I will redeem all this on Percy's head,
And in the closing of some glorious day
Be bold to tell you that I am your son,
When I will wear a garment all of blood,
And stain my favours in a bloody mask,
Which, wash'd away, shall scour my shame with it.
…
This in the name of God I promise here,
The which if He be pleas'd I shall perform,
I do beseech your Majesty may salve
The long-grown wounds of my intemperance.

(III.ii.132–56)

The repentance of the Prince and reconciliation with his father effect a transformation both in his public estimation and the area of imagery that surrounds him. Whereas Hotspur continues to think of him as 'the nimble-footed madcap Prince of Wales / [Who] daft the world aside / And bid it pass' (IV.i.95–7), Vernon, who has seen Hal after his amendment, describes him in very different terms:

I saw young Harry with his beaver on,
His cushes on his thighs, gallantly arm'd,
Rise from the ground like feather'd Mercury,
And vaulted with such ease into his seat
As if an angel dropp'd down from the clouds
To turn and wind a fiery Pegasus,
And witch the world with noble horsemanship.

(IV.i.104–10)

Here the image of Hal as angel is in striking contrast to the field of reference of the tavern scenes, reinforcing audience awareness of the didactic pattern underlying the play, while the subsequent victory of the Prince over Hotspur completes the redemptive cycle, with right conduct in the wordly sphere leading to temporal, and by implication spiritual, success.

The action of *1 Henry IV* is thus firmly located by the dramatist within the context of a familiar story, and that story's ethical and spiritual ramifications are pointedly evoked in the course of the play. The audience is consequently encouraged to match the events of the drama with those of the conventional tale, and to anticipate the direction the action will take. As noted above, until the close of I.ii the expectations raised by the recognition of the tradition within which the playwright is operating are largely confirmed. The conventional opposition is set up between provident and improvident sons, while Hal's lifestyle in the tavern corresponds with that attributed to him both on the stage and in historical accounts. The soliloquy concluding I.ii comes, therefore, as a very considerable surprise. Poins asks Falstaff to leave him alone with the Prince, promising that he will persuade Hal to join them in a projected robbery, and he and the Prince then plan to rob the robbers themselves. An elaborate 'jest' (I.ii.180) is thus set up in which the two conspirators, and by extension the audience, look forward to 'the incomprehensible lies' the 'fat rogue' will tell at supper (180–1). The tone of the scene is lighthearted, but an instantaneous change occurs when Poins, too, leaves the stage. Left to himself, Hal discloses that his attitudes are not what those around him suppose them to be:

> I know you all, and will awhile uphold
> The unyok'd humour of your idleness.
> Yet herein will I imitate the sun,
> Who doth permit the base contagious clouds
> To smother up his beauty from the world,
> That, when he please again to be himself,
> Being wanted he may be more wonder'd at
> By breaking through the foul and ugly mists
> Of vapours that did seem to strangle him.
> If all the year were playing holidays,
> To sport would be as tedious as to work;
> But when they seldom come, they wish'd-for come,
> And nothing pleaseth but rare accidents:
> So when this loose behaviour I throw off,
> And pay the debt I never promised,
> By how much better than my word I am,
> By so much shall I falsify men's hopes;
> And like bright metal on a sullen ground,
> My reformation, glitt'ring o'er my fault,

Shall show more goodly, and attract more eyes
Than that which hath no foil to set it off.
I'll so offend, to make offence a skill,
Redeeming time when men think least I will.

                                                            (I.ii.190–212)

What Hal reveals here is that contrary to audience assumption he is not a prodigal at all. Far from being corrupted by his companions, he is using them for his own ends, and is fully aware of their baseness. His dissolute lifestyle is not the product of youthful susceptibility to the pleasures of the world, but a deliberate strategy, designed to ease his path to the throne. Similarly, the reformation to which he looks forward is not a return to the path of virtue but an exercise in the manipulation of public opinion. By relieving the fears of his future subjects and exceeding their expectations he hopes to win their admiration and allegiance. Shakespeare's central figure, in short, is not a prodigal prince, but a prince pretending to be a prodigal, and this 'alternative' treatment of the inherited story transforms the significance of the tale.

The revelation of Hal's true attitudes has a retrospective impact on the scenes already witnessed. Whereas the audience has hitherto regarded Henry IV as the conventional father grieved by the dangerous folly of a dissolute son, their perspective alters with the perception that he is operating upon a wholly invalid set of assumptions. Similarly, the easy camaraderie of the preceding tavern scene is significantly undercut by the recognition that the Prince is playing a part, and that he sees the companions he has joked with in terms of baseness and contagion. At the same time, the superior knowledge acquired by the audience in this scene opens up a gap in subsequent episodes between the perceptions of those inside and outside the play world. The audience is continually aware, for example, that Hotspur is wholly mistaken in his assessment of the character of his opponent (cf. I.iii.225–30), while the scene in which Hal and Falstaff act out the roles of King and Prince becomes heavily ironic when Hal, seemingly in the character of his father, affirms his intention to banish Falstaff (effected in the second part of the play). The reconciliation scene, too, between the King and his 'erring' heir fails to carry for the audience the unequivocal joy and relief experienced by the father figure. Henry's admonitions with regard to Hal's behaviour are robbed of their conventional weight by the evident shrewdness of the Prince's conduct, while Hal's attribution of the image he has cultivated to 'base newsmongers' (III.ii.25) and his seeming reformation, constitute the culmination of a strategy, rather than a recognition of the social and spiritual danger of the course he has pursued. Whereas for Vernon the Prince who emerges from the tavern is recreated in the likeness of a god (cf. IV.i.106), for the members of the audience he brings to fruition the first stage of a policy initiated before the start of the play.

The change that Shakespeare effects in the motives underlying the conduct of the Prince serve to locate the drama in a very different world from that evoked by the traditional story. The Prodigal Son plays, Moralities and early Histories all project a moral universe, in which virtuous action leads inexorably to earthly and heavenly reward, and misconduct to penury and damnation. The aim of the dramatist is to elevate and warn, and the relationship between probity and success and civil and divine order is assumed throughout. An ideal world is thus set before the audience in that human affairs are presented not as they are, but as they ought to be. Shakespeare's version of the prodigal son story is altogether more disturbing in that success is no longer dependent upon right conduct. Hal is reconciled with his father and engages the admiration of all classes not because he repents of his errors, and discards the sins of his youth, but because he is cleverer than those around him, and is able to manipulate public opinion to his own advantage. In terms of absolute morality, his conduct throughout is open to censure. He distances himself from the court and thus occasions his father anxiety on both a personal and a political level not because he is misled by Falstaff but because he sees notoriety as a means of furthering his own ambitions, while he exploits the trust of his (albeit corrupt and self-seeking) tavern companions. Rather than being ensnared by others, he engages in a deliberate campaign of deception, presenting a false appearance to the world at large. Nevertheless, the audience is left in no doubt that though the actions of the Prince may be morally questionable, they will lead not to failure but success. His career in the tavern, for example, ensures him the wholehearted loyalty of the lower orders who come to regard him as one of themselves, cf:

> ... I am sworn brother to a leash of drawers, and can call them all by their christen names ... They take it already upon their salvation, that though I be but Prince of Wales, yet I am the king of courtesy ... a Corinthian, a lad of mettle, a good boy (by the Lord, so they call me!), and when I am King of England I shall command all the good lads in Eastcheap,
>
> (II.v.6–14)

while his seeming return to the path of virtue wins the admiration of his own class, cf:

> Vernon. And which became him like a prince indeed,
> He made a blushing cital of himself,
> And chid his truant youth with such a grace
> As if he master'd there a double spirit
> Of teaching and of learning instantly.
> There did he pause: but let me tell the world –
> If he outlive the envy of this day,
> England did never owe so sweet a hope
> So much misconstru'd in his wantonness.

(V.ii.60–8)

The new status he achieves in the course of the play is signalled by an incident in the final scene concerning the leader of the Scottish forces, the Earl of Douglas. In I.ii Hotspur's soldiership and position as the glass of honour is suggested by the fact that he has taken Douglas's eldest son (among others) prisoner, while his quarrel with the King is initiated by his refusal to yield him up to his messenger. At the close of the play it is revealed that Hal holds Douglas himself prisoner, thus surpassing Hotspur's achievement, and his new social prestige is indicated by the King's readiness to allow him to dispose of him as he wishes (V.v.17–24).

Just as the equation between right conduct and worldly success is subverted in the course of the play, so too is the relationship between right conduct and education. The prodigals of the hybrid Moralities are faced with a choice between study and the pleasures of the world, invariably rejecting the former in favour of the latter. Knowledge is thus linked with virtue, and becomes associated with the path to heaven. The education theme is carried over into Shakespeare's play, but it is now the tavern which is the place of study. Hal abandons the court to learn about his future subjects, and in doing so acquires skills that would once have placed him upon the road to damnation, cf:

> Poins. Where hast been, Hal?
> Prince. With three or four loggerheads, amongst three or fourscore
> hogsheads. I have sounded the very base-string of humility.
> Sirrah, I am sworn brother to a leash of drawers ... They call
> drinking deep 'dyeing scarlet', and when you breathe in your
> watering they cry 'Hem!' and bid you 'Play it off!' To conclude
> I am so good a proficient in one quarter of an hour that I can drink
> with any tinker in his own language during my life.

(II.iv.3–19)

Here associating with those of a lower class, learning the language and customs of the uneducated, sharing pleasures conventionally associated with the overthrow of reason, becomes a pathway to social preferment, with the acquisition of knowledge divorced from progress towards the divine.

Yet more disturbing, perhaps, for a contemporary audience than the severance of right conduct from worldly success and education from the path of virtue is the deliberate exploitation by the Prince of these conventional moral and spiritual equations. Hal is not simply a prince pretending to be a prodigal, he is also a royal politician, self-consciously evoking religious beliefs and ethical absolutes in order to serve his own ambitions. The terms in which he describes the strategy that he has devised to secure the loyalty of his future subjects draw very deliberately on the prodigal son story, and exhibit a conscious determination to exploit public familiarity with its repentance/redemption process, cf:

> So when this loose behaviour I throw off,
> And pay the debt I never promised,
> By how much better than my word I am,
> By so much shall I falsify men's hopes;
> And like bright metal on a sullen ground,
> My reformation, glitt'ring o'er my fault,
> Shall show more goodly, and attract more eyes
> Than that which hath no foil to set it off.
> I'll so offend, to make offence a skill,
> Redeeming time when men think least I will.

(I.ii.203–12)

Here, the terminology Hal uses would have left a sixteenth-century audience in no doubt of the Biblical parable that he has elected to re-enact. The references to his 'loose behaviour' and to the repayment of debts associate him with prodigal living, while the terms 'reformation' and 'redeeming' locate the course he is pursuing within the context of Christian thought. Hal's success in persuading his subjects of his transformation thus depends upon the conscious manipulation of the religious convictions of his age, and the extent of his achievement is indicated by Vernon's description of him before the final battle as an 'angel' (IV.i.108).

While the cynicism implicit in the conscious expoitation of individuals and ethical assumptions should, theoretically, alienate those outside the play world, in Shakespeare's alternative Prodigal Son play the Prince's heterodox attitudes invite a considerable measure of respect. Those ranged around Hal are not the black and white representatives of the polarities of homiletic drama, and their behaviour offers some justification for the course of action he elects to pursue. The King is not simply a grieving father, but a usurper, responsible for the death of the previous king, and it is entirely necessary for Hal to distance himself from him if his own reign is not to be tainted by the means through which the throne was obtained. His tavern companions are not embodiments of selfless friendship but anarchic wastrels who hope to benefit by his accession, and his determination to banish Falstaff can only be of profit to the realm. Similarly, Hotspur and his allies are not the purgers of a corrupt order, but rebels dissatisfied with the king they helped to instal, and there can be no peace in the kingdom until a stronger magnetism emerges to replace that of Hotspur's personality. In the world of *1 Henry IV* no party embodies right conduct, and the Prince's self-imposed detachment and his strategy to unite the divided kingdom have the virtue of offering the hope of a new beginning. At the same time, some aspects of Hal's personality are inherently likeable, engaging the sympathies of those inside and outside the play world. His quickness of mind makes him a fit companion for Falstaff, while his energy and clear-sightedness invite a degree of audience admiration. Conversely, while the failings of those around him supply a degree of justification for the conduct of the Prince, his own behaviour elicits sympathy for those he makes his instruments. Whereas in the conventional monitory dramas of the period the false friends who bring about the seduction of youth are patently vicious, Falstaff and his tavern companions are not so easily categorized. Hal's acute intelligence defuses the danger represented by their conduct, allowing a more sympathetic view of tavern life, and creating a sense of uneasiness when the trust that they place in him is abused. In the scene in which Hal baits the drawer, Francis, for example, the audience is not gratified by the spectacle of a purveyor of alcohol being tormented for the wickedness of his trade, but concerned at the sight of an overworked apprentice being harried by a man he admires (cf. II.iv.29–75).

It will be clear from the above that the universe in which *1 Henry IV* is set is at once more complex and in some respects less comfortable than the world of the dramatic tradition to which the play ultimately belongs. Rather than presenting an ethical universe in which moral absolutes are clearly differentiated, Shakespeare is concerned with the realities of the day-to-day world in which vice and virtue are not always readily distinguished, human beings are a mixture of good and bad impulses, and intelligence, not right conduct, ensures worldly success. Rather than inculcating a set of moral lessons, the play consequently questions, or interrogates, the assumptions underlying the traditional story, exposing the gap between the implied Christian ideal and political actuality. In the course of the action the members of the audience are faced with such issues as whether the end justifies the means, whether the old are inevitably wiser than the young, if immoral conduct does in fact lead to worldly failure, and whether vice is always and inherently unattractive. The spectator is thus transformed from a passive recipient of instruction into an active participant in the play's events, encouraged to judge, take sides, and experience the difficulty of formulating judgements in a world in which 'good' and 'bad' may not be identical in the political and personal arenas.

Shakespeare's play is thus concerned, fundamentally, not with piety but with power, and it is this aspect of the play that has attracted the notice of much contemporary criticism. Many of the new approaches to literary studies that have emerged in recent years are also concerned with political issues, New Historicism and Cultural Materialism in particular focussing upon the relationship between ideology, social institutions and class. The New Historicist perspective is essentially a pessimistic one, exploring the way in which literary works are located within and function to sustain an existing social system, while Cultural Materialism is more optimistic in that it is concerned with sites of resistance to dominant institutions and is interested in forces of change. Shakespeare's political prodigal lends himself to both types of discourse, and the very different ways in which his story may be viewed from a twentieth-century perspective affords some indication of the complex nature of the interaction that the dramatist sets up between his alternative and inherited tales.

For the New Historicist critic, subversion is always contained by a dominant ideology and legitimacy is not a matter of right or linear succession but the ability to appropriate and secure the symbols of authority. Power is thus dependent 'not on legitimacy but legitimation',[11] and *1 Henry IV* exhibits a number of examples of this process at work. Henry IV himself is a rebel, who has deposed the previous monarch with the assistance of his fellow peers. Though he has no absolute right to the throne, once he is installed as king he takes on all the trappings of sovereignty (the royal 'we', the role of defender of Christendom, etc.), marginalizing those who were formerly his allies, but who now resist his authority, by terming them 'rebels'. A 'rebel' is thus not one who dis-

---

11. Graham Holderness (ed.) (1992) *Shakespeare's History Plays: Richard II to Henry V*, New Casebooks, Macmillan, p. 12.

sents from the rule of a divinely ordained monarch but one who opposes those who wield the greatest power, while his defeat contributes, in turn, to the process of legitimation in that it reinforces the position (and thus helps to sanction the authority) of the dominant group. Hal's career may be seen as a much more striking example of this concept of appropriation. At the opening of the play his conduct appears to be 'oppositional', in that he associates with those whose way of life offers a challenge to the Christian world order. In fact, however, as he reveals in I.ii he is engaged in harnessing, or containing, the forces of subversion as a means of legitimizing his own authority. By reenacting the tale of the Prodigal Son, he not only secures the loyalty of those who offer a challenge to the socioreligious orthodoxies which underpin the power structure, he also locates himself within an ideological framework that serves to associate him with the divine and thus authenticates his fitness to reign. Subversion is thus encouraged in order to be exploited, and religion becomes an instrument of power politics. Hal is thus not simply a prince pretending to be a prodigal, he is a prince who takes over the prodigal tradition as a means of legitimating his own rule.

For the Cultural Materialist critic, by contrast, Shakespeare's alternative tale carries a rather different significance. By departing from the black and white oppositions of the inherited story the dramatist has shifted the focus of attention from the moral of the Biblical parable to the individuals caught up in the process, and this is particularly apparent in his treatment of the play's 'oppositional' voices. Whereas the righteous of the inherited hybrid Moralities were frequently presented as flawed, the corrupt were irredeemably vicious, unequivocal embodiments of the impulses drawing man along the path to damnation. Shakespeare's roisterers, by contrast, are more complex, as noted above, than the false friends from whom they derive, and Falstaff in particular enunciates a philosophy that not only challenges the dominant ideology but commands a measure of audience respect. His famous discourse on honour (V.i.127–41), for example, undermines not only the chivalric code that Hotspur embodies, but the entire relationship between signified and signifier. 'Honour' he decides is simply a word, 'air' (135), 'a mere scutcheon' (i.e. heraldic ensign) (140–1), and the divorce he sets up between the word itself and the meaning imposed upon it by the dominant power group has far-reaching implications in relation to other concepts invoked in the play (e.g. 'rebel'). At the same time, the world of the tavern offers a carnivalesque alternative to the life of the court with its own very different value system, cf:

Fal[staff]. Marry then sweet wag, when thou art king let not us that are
   squires of the night's body be called thieves of the day's beauty: let us
   be Diana's foresters, gentlemen of the shade, minions of the moon;
   and let men say we be men of good government, being governed as
   the sea is, by our noble and chaste mistress the moon, under whose
   countenance we steal.

(I.ii.23–9)

and the subculture's invitation to 'be merry' (II.iv.275) is as potent as
their superiors' call to arms ('O let the hours be short, / Till fields, and
blows, and groans applaud our sport!' I.iii.295–6).

   Where the conventional Prodigal Son play projected a single unequivocal meaning, Shakespeare's play thus enacts more than one story
simultaneously, and this plurality of meaning is itself of particular interest
to the socio-political wing of contemporary criticism. Where
Shakespeare's history plays were once seen as enacting a progress towards
an ideal nation state defined in terms of the 'Elizabethan world picture',[12]
it is now recognized that Elizabethan thought was not as monolithic as
was once presumed and that the experiences of different groups within
society are not identical. English history seen from the perspective of a
woman is not the same as history seen from the perspective of a man, nor
are the histories of the different classes identical. The version of the
Prodigal Son story enacted in *1 Henry IV* confirms this diversity of
human experience. The King's tale is not the same as Hal's, for example,
and both are different from Hotspur's or Falstaff's. Henry sees his son's
career in terms of the conventional process of misconduct, repentance
and success, Hal engages in a political manoeuvre, Hotspur is concerned
to right a personal and public wrong, while Falstaff thinks he is hail-fel-
low-well-met with the heir to the throne and that he can use him for his
own ends. The King's history is one of careful consolidation, Falstaff's
(ultimately) a record of exploitation and rejection, Hotspur's one of dis-
appointment, and Hal's the triumph of political pragmatism.

   While the multiple experiences of *1 Henry IV* subvert the concept of
history as a monolithic process, however, the larger cycle of plays to
which *1 Henry IV* belongs and in which Shakespeare traces the career of
his prodigal prince maps the way in which 'official' history is made. I.ii
of *1 Henry IV* reveals the mechanism through which Hal hopes to

12. The view is particularly associated with the work of E.M.W. Tillyard in his (1943)
   The Elizabethan World Picture, Chatto and Windus.

secure his insecure succession, and it is clear by the close of the play that his strategy will be a success. As noted above, though the audience is aware throughout that the Prince is playing a part, that he is never truly a prodigal, and does not in fact reform, those within the play world are convinced that they have witnessed his conversion, and he thus gains their admiration and respect. This process is reiterated, moreover, in *2 Henry IV*, and the opening of *Henry V* bears witness to the potency of the myth he has created. Hal has, in effect, written his own history, providing a 'state' view of his own past that authenticates his right to the throne. The speakers here are churchmen, and their approving recapitulation of the Prince's reformation is an index of Hal's success in locating his rule within the framework of Christian ideology:

> Cant[erbury]. The king is full of grace and fair regard.
> Ely. And a true lover of the holy Church.
> Cant. The courses of his youth promis'd it not.
> The breath no sooner left his father's body,
> But that his wildness, mortified in him,
> Seem'd to die too; yea, at that very moment,
> Consideration like an angel came,
> And whipp'd th'offending Adam out of him,
> Leaving his body as a Paradise,
> T'envelop and contain celestial spirits.
> Never was such a sudden scholar made;
> Never came reformation in a flood,
> With such a heady currance, scouring faults;
> Nor ever Hydra-headed wilfulness
> So soon did lose his seat – and all at once –
> As in this king.
> Ely.   We are blessed in the change.
> Cant. Hear him but reason in divinity,
> And, all-admiring, with an inward wish
> You would desire the king were made a prelate:
> Hear him debate of commonwealth affairs,
> You would say it hath been all in all his study:
> List his discourse of war, and you shall hear
> A fearful battle render'd you in music:
> Turn him to any cause of policy,
> The Gordian knot of it he will unloose,
> Familiar as his garter; that, when he speaks,
> The air, a charter'd libertine, is still,
> And the mute wonder lurketh in men's ears,
> To steal his sweet and honey'd sentences;

So that the art and practic part of life
Must be the mistress to this theoric:
Which is a wonder how his grace should glean it,
Since his addiction was to courses vain;
His companies unletter'd, rude and shallow;
His hours fill'd up with riots, banquets, sports;
And never noted in him any study,
Any retirement, any sequestration
From open haunts and popularity.

(Henry V, I.i.22–59)

Here the complex web of actuality has been simplified, and history re-written to conform to the paradigmatic process. The companions of the Prince's youth (which must include Falstaff) have become 'unletter'd rude and shallow', his reformation is an instantaneous one (cf. 'at that very moment') and is a matter of piety rather than pragmatism (cf. 'Leaving his body as a Paradise, / T'envelop and contain celestial spirits'). Where Hal's education was undertaken in the tavern, his new-written history makes his learning the product of his reformation (cf. 'Never was such a sudden scholar made'), while the spiritual rather than political nature of his transformation is accentuated by the profound understanding he displays of 'divinity'. The shrewd Prince of the Boar's Head has become the conventional erring young man of the hybrid Moralities, his conversion ensuring wise government and success on the battlefield, while endowing his kingship with divine sanction. The 'alternative' tale has given place, once again, to the 'official' version of the story, the account that will find its way into the chronicles, and will one day be re-enacted in *The Famous Victories of Henry V*. The tale of the prodigal son, in short, has come full circle, but the timeless process that has been enacted in the course of its passage through Shakespeare's work is political rather than spiritual, and may be seen as a parable for our own time.

Chapter 2

King John and the Tale of the Bastard Son

Therefore know you gentlemen ... that having had in lawful marriage, of a mother fit to bear royal children, this son ... and so enjoyed the expectations in the world of him, till he was grown to justify their expectations (so as I needed envy no father for the chief comfort of mortality, to leave another oneself after me) I was carried by a bastard son of mine ... first to mislike, then to hate, lastly to destroy, to do my best to destroy, this son ... undeserving destruction. What ways he used to bring me to it, if I should tell you, I should tediously trouble you with as much poisonous hypocrisy, desperate fraud, smooth malice, hidden ambition, and smiling envy as in any living person could be harboured ... The conclusion is that I gave order to some servants of mine, whom I thought apt for such charities as my self, to lead him out into a forest, and there to kill him.

But those thieves (bettered natured to my son than myself) spared his life, letting him go, to learn to live poorly, which he did, giving himself to be a private soldier in a country here by. But, as he was ready to be greatly advanced for some noble pieces of service which he did, he heard news of me who (drunk in my affection to that unlawful and unnatural son of mine) suffered my self so to be governed by him, that all favours and punishments passed by him, all offices, and places of importance distributed to his favourites, so that ere I was aware, I had left myself nothing but the name of a king, which he shortly weary of too, with many indignities ... threw me out of my seat, and put out my eyes; and then (proud in his tyranny) let me go, neither imprisoning, nor killing me, but rather delighting to make me feel my misery ... And as he came to the crown by so unjust means as unjustly he kept it, by force of stranger soldiers in citadels, the nests of tyranny and murderers of liberty, disarming all his own countrymen, that no man durst show himself a wellwisher of mine.... Till this son of mine (God knows worthy of a more virtuous and more fortunate father) forgetting my abominable wrongs, not reckoning danger, and neglecting the present good way he was in doing himself good, came hither ... But by and by ... *Plexirtus* (so was the bastard called) came thither with forty horse, only of purpose to murder this brother, of whose coming he had soon advertisement, and thought no eyes of sufficient credit in such a matter but his own, and therefore came himself to be actor and spectator ... But the young Prince (though not otherwise armed but with a sword) how falsely soever he was dealt with by others, would not betray himself, but bravely drawing it out, made the death of the first that assaulted him ... Then the match had been so ill-made for *Plexirtus* that his ill-led life and worse gotten honour should have tumbled together to destruction had there not come in *Tydeus* and *Telenor*, with forty or fifty in their suit, to the defence of *Plexirtus* ... [and] carried away that ungrateful master of theirs to a place of security ... But *Plexirtus*, finding that, if nothing else, famine would at last bring him to destruction, thought better by humbleness to creep where by pride he could not march. For certainly so had nature formed him, and the exercise of craft conformed him to all turnings of sleights, that though no man had less goodness in his soul than he, no man could better find the places whence arguments might grow of goodness to another; though no man felt less pity, no man could tell better how to stir pity; no man more impudent to deny where proofs were not manifest; no man more ready to confess with a repenting manner of aggravating his own evil where denial would but make the fault fouler ... So fell out of it that ... ere long he had not only gotten pity but pardon, and if not an excuse of the fault past, yet an opinion of a future amendment.

Tales turning upon the perfidy of an illegitimate son (exemplified here from Sir Philip Sidney's *The Countess of Pembroke's Arcadia*)[1] are common in Renaissance literature and the issue of bastardy is frequently raised on the Elizabethan-Jacobean stage. Of the plays performed between the opening of the first purpose-built playhouses in the late 1570s and the closing of the theatres in 1642, approximately a fifth reveal an interest in the illegitimate condition, a significant proportion employing the birth of a child outside marriage as a motive for action or source of complication in either main or sub plots.[2] The treatment of bastardy across this wide spectrum of plays is, moreover, remarkably uniform. From Hughes' *The Misfortunes of Arthur* (1588) to Nabbes' *The Unfortunate Mother* (1639?), illegitimacy is viewed as both a personal and familial disaster, while the bastard is presented as evil by nature, a portrayal founded upon the assumption that those born outside the bonds of wedlock are inherently

---

1. Book II, Chapter 10. The extract quoted is based upon the edition in Geoffrey Bullough (1957–75) *Narrative and Dramatic Sources of Shakespeare*, vol. vii, Routledge and Kegan Paul, pp. 404–8, but spelling and punctuation have been modernized.
2. See my unpublished MA thesis, 'The Bastard in Elizabethan and Jacobean Drama', University of Liverpool, 1964, pp. 227ff.

anti-social. In *Andromana, or The Merchant's Wife* (by 'J.S.', 1642–60), for example, the King declares that his son's ungoverned behaviour would be comprehensible if he were base born rather than legitimate, cf:

> Ungracious boy,
> Hadst thou been offspring of a sinful bed,
> Thou might have claim'd adultery as inheritance;
> Lust would have been thy kinsman,
> And what enormity thy looser life
> Could have been guilty of, had found excuse
> In an unnatural conception;
>
> (I.iv)[3]

while the second of Fletcher's *Four Plays or Moral Representations in One* (c.1608–13) sums up the pervasive attitude towards birth outside marriage in Ferdinand's lament over a (seemingly) illegitimate child:

> Poor infant, what's become of thee? thou knowest not
> The woe thy parents brought thee to. Dear Earth,
> Bury this close in thy sterility;
> Be barren to this seed, let it not grow!
> For if it do, 'twill bud no violet,
> Nor gilly-flower, but wild brier, or rank rue,
> Unsavoury and hurtful.
>
> (Scene v)[4]

The stance of the bastard towards his society[5] is almost invariably one of resentment – towards the father responsible for the outcast nature of his birth, towards those within the family group more favourably circumstanced than himself (most usually his legitimate siblings), and ultimately towards the community as a whole. Mordred in *The Misfortunes of Arthur*, for example, brings about the destruction of his father's kingdom; Don John in Shakespeare's *Much Ado About Nothing* (1598) sows dissention among his brother's courtiers; Spurio in Middleton's(?) *The Revenger's Tragedy* is a 'hate all' (I.ii.201),[6] who cuckolds his father and kills his step-brother; while Antipater in

3. Quoted from W. Carew Hazlitt (ed.) (1874) *A Select Collection of Old English Plays, Originally published by Robert Dodsley*, vol. xiv, 4th edn, Reeves and Turner. (Lines are unnumbered.)
4. Quoted from George Darley (ed.) (1866) *The Works of Beaumont and Fletcher*, vol. ii, George Routledge and Sons. (Lines are unnumbered.)
5. Illegitimate daughters are rare in these plays.
6. Quoted from R.A. Foakes (ed.) (1966) *The Revenger's Tragedy*, Methuen. All subsequent references are to this edition.

Markham and Sampson's *Herod and Antipater* (c.1622) plots against his entire family, bringing each of its members to a violent end. The characterization of these figures, moreover, for all the diversity of plays in which they appear, is strikingly similar. The majority, like Sidney's Plexirtus, are clever (cf. Edricus in Anon, *Edmund Ironside*, 1590–1600), highly manipulative (cf. Codigune in R.A's *The Valiant Welshman*, 1610–15), ambitious (cf. Henry of Trastomare in Wentworth Smith's *The Hector of Germany*, 1614–15), cruel (cf. Markham and Sampson's Antipater) and lascivious (cf. Beaufort in Chettle, Day and Haughton's *The Blind Beggar of Bednal Green*, 1600). Liberated from conventional moral restraints by their exclusion from the natural order, their creed is self-sufficiency, expounded most lucidly by Shakespeare's Edmund:

> Thou, Nature, art my goddess; to thy law
> My services are bound. Wherefore should I
> Stand in the plague of custom, and permit
> The curiosity of nations to deprive me,
> For that I am some twelve or fourteen moonshines
> Lag of a brother? Why bastard? Wherefore base?
> When my dimensions are as well compact,
> My mind as generous, and my shape as true,
> As honest madam's issue? Why brand they us
> With base? with baseness? bastardy? base, base?
> Who in the lusty stealth of nature take
> More composition and fierce quality
> Than doth, within a dull, stale, tired bed,
> Go to th'creating a whole tribe of fops,
> Got 'tween asleep and wake? Well then,
> Legitimate Edgar, I must have your land:
> Our father's love is to the bastard Edmund
> As to th'legitimate. Fine word, "legitimate"!
> Well, my legitimate, if this letter speed,
> And my invention thrive, Edmund the base
> Shall top th'legitimate – : I grow, I prosper;
> Now, gods, stand up for bastards!
>
> (*King Lear*, I.ii.1–22)

While the bastard son is almost invariably presented as degenerate, the father who foisted his unnatural condition upon him is both implicated in his guilt and frequently punished through his offspring for his own crime. The viciousness of those born outside marriage is seen not merely as a consequence of their unnatural status, but as an inheritance, in that their fathers were vicious before them. This interchange of guilt between the generations, constantly reiterated by the old King in Sidney's *Arcadia*, is spelled out in Lyly's *Euphues* (1578), the most popular prose work of the period:

> *That the child should be true born, no bastard*
> First, touching their procreation, it shall seem necessary to
> entreat of whosoever he be that desireth to be the sire of an
> happy son or the father of a fortunate child, let him abstain
> from those women which be ... bare of honesty. For if the mother
> be noted of incontinency or the father of vice, the child will
> either during life be infected with the like crime or the
> treacheries of his parents as ignomy [sic] to him will be
> cast in his teeth. For we commonly call those unhappy children
> which have sprung from unhonest parents ... The guilty conscience of
> a father that trodden awry causeth him to think and suspect
> that his father also went not right, whereby his own behaviour
> is as it were a witness of his own baseness.
>
> (*Euphues:The Anatomy of Wit*)[7]

Numerous plays attest to the bond between the illegitimate child and the erring father. Just as the Old King in Sidney's *Arcadia* is blinded and reduced to penury by the offspring who is the product of his own misconduct, so Shakespeare's Gloucester is brought to recognize that the 'sport' (I.i.23) through which Edmund was conceived was the ultimate source of his own blinding, while the trusting Octavian in *The Valiant Welshman* is ruthlessly murdered by his son Codigune. The initial act of misconduct by the father is frequently compounded, moreover, by the disproportionate degree of affection that he displays towards his illegitimate child, who in turn makes him the instrument of further breaches of the natural order. Thus the Old King in Sidney's *Arcadia* is brought to consent to the death of his virtuous legitimate son (cf. the relationship between Edmund, Gloucester and Edgar in *King Lear*), while Herod comes to recognize that all his unnatural actions have sprung from the promptings of his son Antipater, cf:

---

7. Quoted from Morris William Croll and Harry Clemons (eds) (1964, first published 1916) *Euphues, The Anatomy of Wit: Euphues and his England*, Russell and Russell, p. 114.

O this son,
This bastard son hath only ruined me.
Hell never knew his equal; all my sins
Are but the seeds he planted.

(V.ii.175–8)[8]

The attitudes to bastardy presented in these plays are clearly rooted in the Christian concept of marriage as a divinely ordained institution. In a Christian society to be born outside wedlock is to be born outside the moral order, brought into the world through an act of sin. In the words of Bishop Launcelot Andrewes (1555–1626), those born of an act of adultery 'shall not be accounted as one of the congregation of the Lord,'[9] and are a punishment to their offending parents. The spiritual implications of birth outside marriage loom large in the plays of the period, providing both an explanation for the inherent viciousness of the 'whoreson' and a motive for his resentment. Arbaces, for example, in Beaumont and Fletcher's *A King and No King*, believing himself to be illegitimate, enquires bitterly of his parents for directions to the 'spacious world / Of impious acts' (V.iv.165–6)[10] which they have bequeathed to him, while the Duchess in *The Revenger's Tragedy*, seeking to draw the bastard Spurio into an incestuous relationship with her, elaborates as a perverse incentive on the socio-theological implications of his position:

O what a grief 'tis, that a man should live
But once i'th'world, and then to live a bastard,
The curse o'th'womb, the thief of nature,
Begot against the seventh commandment,
Half-damn'd in the conception, by the justice
Of that unbribed everlasting law.

(I.ii.159–64)

It is not merely the theological framework, however, against which the condition of base birth is defined. The exclusion of the bastard from 'the congregation of the Lord' had legal repercussions during the period that bred further causes of resentment. The definition of the term 'bastard' was complicated in Renaissance England by the administration

---

8. Quoted from Gordon Nicholas Ross (ed.) (1979) *A Critical Edition of The True Tragedy of Herod and Antipater*, Garland Publishing. Spelling and punctuation, however, have been modernized.
9. Quoted from (1846) *A Pattern of Catechistical Doctrine and Other Minor Works*, Library of Anglo-Catholic Theology, Oxford, p. 246.
10. Quoted from Robert K. Turner Jnr (ed.) (1964) *A King and No King*, Regents Renaissance Drama Series, Edward Arnold.

of the law by two authorities – temporal and spiritual – whose positions did not always coincide. In the eyes of the state a man born outside wedlock could not be an heir, while those born within marriage, regardless of paternity, were secure against the imputation of bastardy. In the words of Lord Coke:

> We term them all by the name of bastard that be born out
> of lawful marriage. By the Common Law, if the husband be within
> the four seas, that is, within the jurisdiction of the King
> of England, if the wife hath issue, no proof is to be admitted
> to prove the child a bastard (for in that case *filiatio*
> *non potest probari*) unless the husband hath an apparent
> impossibility of procreation, as if the husband be but eight
> years old, or under the age of procreation, such issue is a bastard
> albeit he be born within marriage. But if the issue be born
> within a month or a day after marriage, between parties of
> lawful age, the child is legitimate.[11]

This definition of the term 'bastard' is a highly significant one. In common law a valid marriage afforded an effective bulwark against the charge of illegitimacy even if the offspring of that marriage was born only moments after the couple's nuptials, if the wife was living in open adultery apart from her husband, or the husband was in Ireland (but still 'within the four seas', i.e within the jurisdiction of the King of England) for the entire period of her pregnancy. Such a bulwark was of crucial importance to those seeking to establish their legitimacy, in that the legal disabilities attendant upon bastardy were severe. Not only could an illegitimate son not inherit his father's property, but he had no place in the family group. In the words of Lord Coke:

> B hath issue a bastard son [but he shall not inherit]
> because in law he is not his issue, for *qui ex damnato*
> *coitu nascuntur inter liberos non computentur ... A*
> bastard is *quasi nullius filius* and can have
> no name of reputation as soon as he is born.[12]

The term *nullius filius* registers not merely the technical uncertainty surrounding the paternity of those born outside the married state, but the exclusion of such individuals from an accepted place within the social group. In civic matters the bastard was regarded as a foreigner, and

11. Sir Edward Coke (1628) *First Part of the Institutes of the Laws of England,* p. 244a.
12. Coke, *First Part of the Institutes of the Laws of England,* p. 3b.

could not be admitted to any guild or corporation,[13] while he was barred by the Church from taking Holy Orders.[14] The natural duties of a child towards a parent were not expected of him,[15] and he was viewed as a member of a family only to the extent that he was forbidden to marry his mother, sister, and so on.

The ecclesiastical courts, by contrast, while equally severe in their stance towards illegitimate birth, focused not merely on marriage in determining the status of a child, but on the question of parenthood. In the eyes of the Church, the offspring of couples who subsequently married were legitimized by their parents' union (a view at variance with the Common Law), while children born within marriage but not fathered by the husband were regarded as illegitimate.[16] Groups of individuals thus existed who were legitimate in the eyes of the Church but not of the State, or the State but not the Church, and the fate of such individuals thus depended upon the court in which they were tried. Further uncertainties were generated, moreover, by the period's relatively informal marriage arrangements. In the eyes of both civil and ecclesiastical authorities a precontract (i.e. an agreement to marry made before witnesses) was sufficient to bind a couple together, and the issue of such precontracts were legitimate in the view of both Church and State. The repudiation of precontracts, however, often for financial reasons, and the subsequent marriage of one of the parties, created a class of individuals who though born after nuptials were nevertheless illegitimate, while the offspring of repudiated (and unproven) precontracts might endure the social stigma of bastardy while being confident (in spiritual terms) of their legitimate state.

The discrepancies between the two systems, together with the importance of legitimacy for both the individual and the social group, afforded fertile ground for Renaissance dramatists (many of whom had legal training) to work with. Not only do a large number of plays turn upon the resentment of those excluded from the community by the circumstances of their birth, but many more exploit the tensions created by Common Law – the divorce between paternity and rights of inheritance, the obligation placed upon a husband to father the child of

---

13. See Wilfrid Hooper (1911) *The Law of Illegitimacy*, Sweet and Maxwell, pp. 32–3.
14. See Hooper, *The Law of Illegitimacy*, p. 27.
15. See Sir William Blackstone and R. Burn (1783) *Commentaries on the Laws of England in Four Books*, Bk 1, 9th edn, W. Strahan, pp. 446–59.
16. See Hooper, *The Law of Illegitimacy*, p. 76.

another man, and the difficulty of proving (or disproving) precontracts. Many of these plays bear witness to a detailed knowledge of legal issues, testifying, perhaps, to a pressing social concern. Dekker's *The Noble Spanish Soldier* (1622), for example, reveals a firm understanding of the law relating to betrothal, and a similar knowledge is exhibited (among many other places) in Shakespeare's *Richard III* (1591–2). The plot of Webster's *The Devil's Law Case* (1617–21) involves a tissue of issues relating to bastardy, while Thomas May's *The Heir* (1620) includes references to the legitimacy of those conceived outside but born within marriage, the validity of precontracts, ecclesiastical jurisdiction over matrimonial cases, and the Church's condemnation of priests who officiated at secret weddings.

A number of plays also involve a formal trial designed to establish a character's legal status, and it is one of the earliest of such dramas – the anonymous two-part play, *The Troublesome Reign of King John* (1591) – that constituted, in all probability, the principal source of Shakespeare's alternative version of the tale of the bastard son. The relationship between *The Troublesome Reign*, and Shakespeare's *The Life and Death of King John* (1595–6?) has long been disputed,[17] but the majority of scholars now accept that the anonymous play precedes the Shakespearian drama rather than being a corrupt off-shoot from it, and it is that view which is adopted here. The similarities between the two plays are extensive, and include a lengthy scene in the first act in which a dispute over inheritance is brought before the King. The litigants are the two sons of Lady Falconbridge, and the matter in dispute is the right to inherit her husband's land. The passage from *The Troublesome Reign* is worth quoting at length in that Shakespeare's departures from it are highly significant in relation to his treatment of the issues raised:

> Essex. Gentlemen, it is the King's pleasure that you dis-
>   cover your griefs, and doubt not but you shall have justice.
> Philip. Please it your Majesty, the wrong is mine; yet
>   will I abide all wrongs, before I once open my mouth to un-
>   rip the shameful slander of my parents, the dishonour of
>   myself, and the wicked dealing of my brother in this princely
>   assembly.

17. For a full discussion of this issue see E.A.J. Honigmann (ed.) (1954) *King John*, The Arden Shakespeare, Methuen, pp. xi–xix; William H. Matchett (ed.) (1966) *Shakespeare: King John*, Signet Classics, New English Library, pp. 153–63; R.L. Smallwood (ed.) (1974) *King John*, New Penguin Shakespeare, pp. 365–74; A.R. Braunmuller (ed.) (1989) *King John*, The Oxford Shakespeare, Clarendon Press, pp. 4–15.

Robert. Then by my Prince his leave shall Robert speak,
　　And tell your Majesty what right I have
　　To offer wrong, as he accounteth wrong.
　　My father (not unknown to your Grace)
　　Receiv'd his spurs of knighthood in the field,
　　At kingly Richard's hands in Palestine,
　　When as the walls of Acon gave him way:
　　His name Sir Robert Fauconbridge of Mountbery.
　　What by succession from his ancestors,
　　And warlike service under England's arms
　　His living did amount to at his death
　　Two thousand marks revenue every year:
　　And this (my Lord) I challenge for my right,
　　As lawful heir to Robert Fauconbridge.
Philip. If first-born son be heir indubitate
　　By certain right of England's ancient law,
　　How should myself make any other doubt,
　　But I am heir to Robert Fauconbridge?
John. Fond youth, to trouble these our princely ears
　　Or make a question in so plain a case:
　　Speak, is this man thine elder brother born?
Robert. Please it, your Grace, with patience for to hear;
　　I not deny but he mine elder is,
　　Mine elder brother too: yet in such sort,
　　As he can make no title to the land.
John. A doubtful tale as ever I did hear,
　　Thy brother and thine elder, and no heir:
　　Explain this dark enigma.
Robert. I grant, my Lord, he is my mother's son,
　　Base born, and base begot, no Fauconbridge.
　　Indeed the world reputes him lawful heir,
　　My father in his life did count him so,
　　And here my mother stands to prove him so:
　　But I, my Lord, can prove, and do aver
　　Both to my mother's shame and his reproach,
　　He is no heir, nor yet legitimate.
　　Then, gracious Lord, let Fauconbridge enjoy
　　The living that belongs to Fauconbridge,
　　And let not him possess another's right.
John. Prove this, the land is thine by England's law.
　　...
Philip. Not for my self, nor for my mother now:
　　But for the honour of so brave a man,

Whom he accuseth with adultery:
Here I beseech your Grace upon my knees,
To count him mad, and so dismiss us hence.
Robert.   Nor mad, nor maz'd, but well advised, I
Charge thee before this royal presence here
To be a bastard to King Richard's self,
Son to your Grace, and brother to your Majesty.
Thus bluntly, and –
Q. Elinor.   Young man thou needst not be ashamed of thy kin,
Nor of thy sire. But forward with thy proof.
Robert.   The proof so plain, the argument so strong,
As that your Highness and these noble Lords,
And all (save those that have no eyes to see)
Shall swear him to be bastard to the King.
First when my father was ambassador
In Germany unto the Emperor,
The King lay often at my father's house;
And all the realm suspected what befell:
And at my father's back return again
My mother was deliver'd as 'tis said,
Six weeks before the account my father made.
But more than this: look but on Philip's face,
His features, actions, and his lineaments,
And all this princely presence shall confess,
He is no other but King Richard's son.
Then gracious Lord, rest he King Richard's son,
And let me rest safe in my father's right,
That am his rightful son and only heir.

(Part I, Scene 1, lines 85–174)[18]

The proofs that Robert advances here are tenuous at best, and the
assembled nobles are quick to point out that his case is without founda-
tion:

John.   Is this thy proof, and all thou hast to say?
Robert.   I have no more, nor need I greater proof.
John.   First, where thou saidst in absence of thy sire
My brother often lodged in his house:
And what of that? Base groom to slander him,
That honoured his ambassador so much,

18. All references to *The Troublesome Reign* are to the edition in Bullough, *Narrative and
Dramatic Sources of Shakespeare*, vol. iv. Spelling and punctuation, however, have been
modernized.

In absence of the man to cheer the wife?
This will not hold, proceed unto the next.
Q. Elinor. Thou sayst she teemed six weeks before her time.
Why good Sir Squire are you so cunning grown
To make account of women's reckonings?
Spit in your hand and to your other proofs:
Many mischances hap in such affairs
To make a woman come before her time.
John. And where thou sayst he looketh like the King
In action, feature, and proportion:
Therein I hold with thee, for in my life
I never saw so lively counterfeit
Of Richard Coeur-de-Lion as in him.
Robert. Then good my Lord, be you indifferent judge,
And let me have my living and my right.
Q. Elinor. Nay hear you sir, you run away too fast:
Know you not, *Omne simile non est idem*?
Or have read in – [sic]. Hark ye good sir,
'Twas thus I warrant, and no otherwise,
She lay with Sir Robert your father, and thought upon
King Richard my son, and so your brother was formed in
this fashion.
Robert. Madam, you wrong me thus to jest it out,
I crave my right: King John as thou art king,
So be thou just, and let me have my right.
John. Why, foolish boy, thy proofs are frivolous,
Nor canst thou challenge anything thereby.

(lines 175–207)

Up to this point in the play the conduct of the trial has been unexceptional. The evidence brought before the King is clearly without force or substance, and John's judgement that it is 'frivolous' is legally sound. Nothing that Robert adduces jeopardizes the security of Philip's legal position, and it is made clear in the course of these exchanges that he has suffered none of the disabilities associated with illegitimate birth. His mother is adamant that he is her husband's son, Sir Robert acknowledged him and accounted him his heir, and his position is unquestioned by the world at large (lines 121–3). In the eyes of the law he is a legitimate member of the community, entitled to both the property and respect due to an elder son. At this point in the action, however, the dramatist violates the realism of his trial scene by turning to the defendants for a judgement on their case. To Robert's dismay, he appeals first to Lady Fauconbridge and then to Philip to affirm the truth regarding Philip's paternity, and both characters maintain initially that Sir Robert was in fact his father. As a final judgement is about to be passed, however, Philip falls into a momentary trance, when he hears a voice telling him that he is born of ancient kings, cf:

> Essex. Philip, speak I say, who was thy father?
> John. Young man! How now? What, art thou in a trance?
> Elinor. Philip, awake! The man is in a dream.
> Philip. *Philippus atauis aedite regibus.*
> What sayst thou? 'Philip, sprung of ancient kings'?
> *Quo me rapit tempestas?*
> What wind of honour blows this fury forth?
> Or whence proceed these fumes of majesty?
> Methinks I hear a hollow echo sound,
> That Philip is the son unto a king:
> The whistling leaves upon the trembling trees
> Whistle in consort I am Richard's son:
> The bubbling murmur of the waters fall,
> Records *Philippus regius filius*:
> Birds in their flight make music with their wings,
> Filling the air with glory of my birth:
> Birds, bubbles, leaves, and mountains, echo, all
> Ring in mine ears, that I am Richard's son.
>
> (lines 238–55)

Clearly, the implication here is of some supernatural force acquainting Philip of his destiny, and it is in response to the promptings of these intimations of his true origins that Philip repudiates Sir Robert and declares himself to be Richard's son. Thus, while on the one hand the legal process that has taken place has liberated him from the social disabilities of the bastard condition, firmly establishing his legitimacy in the legal sense, the quasi-supernatural force that prompts him to repudiate Sir Robert frees him from the spiritual implications of 'base' birth, establishing him, not as a malignant outsider, but as the exceptional son of a legendary father, who has chosen his own (heroic) path in life.

The sense that Philip has been brought from obscurity to prominence by some supernatural force is heightened by the context in which the trial scene is set. The play opens with the French King's demand that John yield his throne to his nephew Arthur and the entrance of the Fauconbridge brothers is preceded by John's announcement that he intends to answer the challenge by fortifying his French possessions. Philip (as he is largely known throughout) thus emerges at a time of

national crisis, and his resemblance to his father is constantly emphasized. He challenges Lymoges for the lion skin, for example, once
possessed by Coeur-de-Lion, wins it from him, and subsequently wears
it (cf. Part I Scene iv, lines 700–15). It is not merely England's heroic
past with which he is identified, however. *The Troublesome Reign of King
John* treats the political confusion of the early years of the thirteenth
century from an anti-Catholic standpoint, and Philip's role in this context is a significant one. John, while acknowledging himself to be too
flawed a man to free England from the yoke of Rome, is presented,
nevertheless, as a precursor of Henry VIII – attempting to resist the
Pope's authority (cf. his refusal to confirm the appointment of Stephen
Langton as Archbishop of Canterbury in Part I, Scene v), to purge the
realm of corrupt religious institutions (cf. the pillaging of the wealth of
the monasteries that takes place in Part I, Scene xi), and to re-establish a
sense of national identity (cf. Part II, Scene ii, lines 222ff. in which he
laments the disorder into which the realm has fallen). Philip is the
instrument of these political/religious objectives, and is far more effective in pursuing them than the King himself. His directness stands in
stark contrast to the Cardinal's deviousness throughout, while he acts as
John's agent in divesting the monasteries of their wealth and exposing
their corruption. It is he who maintains against the rebellious nobles that
the Pope cannot depose an annointed King (cf. Part II, Scene iii, lines
446–88), who leads John's forces against a Catholic-inspired foreign
invasion, and finally closes the play with a declaration of the invinci-
bility of an independent, united England.

Throughout the turmoil into which Philip is plunged in the course of
the play it is his lineage, rather than his illegitimacy, that the dramatist
stresses. He is an outsider in his society only in the sense that he is the
representative of an old order, and the associations that surround him
serve to link him with the offspring of classical deities (cf. Philip's own
frequent classical allusions, e.g. Part I, Scene ii, lines 556ff.) rather than
with the unfortunate products of more mundane illicit unions.
Shakespeare's *King John*, by contrast, while drawing heavily on the
earlier play, places far greater emphasis upon the bastardy of
Faulconbridge, exploiting the connotations that conventionally cluster
around the figure of the illegitimate son.

From the very outset, Shakespeare's version of the conflicts of the
early years of the thirteenth century centres upon the concept of
legitimacy. While *The Troublesome Reign of King John* looks back to
the anti-Catholic polemic of the mid-sixteenth century Morality

play,[19] Shakespeare's drama is concerned with an issue of particular concern in the Elizabethan period (and of pressing interest in the 1590s), the criteria governing lawful succession.[20] Whereas the anonymous play opens with a speech by Elinor presenting John as a 'second hope' of her womb who will prove a fit successor to his brother Richard, thus aligning the audience with him before the abrupt demand from the French that he should renounce his throne to Arthur, *King John* begins with a dispute regarding the legality of John's succession:

> K.John. Now, say, Chatillon, what would France with us?
> Chat. Thus, after greeting, speaks the King of France
>   In my behaviour to the majesty,
>   The borrow'd majesty, of England here.
> Elea[nor]. A strange beginning: 'borrow'd majesty'!
> K.John. Silence, good mother; hear the embassy.
> Chat. Philip of France, in right and true behalf
>   Of thy deceased brother Geoffrey's son,
>   Arthur Plantagenet, lays most lawful claim
>   To this fair island and the territories:
>   To Ireland, Poictiers, Anjou, Touraine, Maine,
>   Desiring thee to lay aside the sword
>   Which sways usurpingly these several titles,
>   And put the same into young Arthur's hand,
>   Thy nephew and right royal sovereign.

(I.i.1–15)

The phrase 'a strange beginning' could be seen as appropriate not merely to Chatillon's speech but the play as a whole. The audience is confronted with a situation in which an older man is accused of withholding property from a younger, an improbable situation in a society governed by the law of primogeniture, and might well feel, like King John in the anonymous play, that they are faced with some 'dark enigma'. The nationalistic impulse triggered by a confrontation between England and France would have disposed a sixteenth-century spectator in all probability to dismiss Chatillon's claim as a foreign fiction, but the uneasy atmosphere generated by the opening is heightened when Eleanor herself concedes, after Chatillon's departure, that the French position is in fact a just one. While John invokes 'Our strong possession and our right' (I.i.39) in support of his cause, Eleanor counters:

19. For a comparable use of the reign of King John as a vehicle for anti-Catholic propaganda see John Bale's hybrid Moral-History, *King Johan* (*A* version 1538, *B* version 1558–62).
20. See below pp. 54ff.

Your strong possession much more than your right,
Or else it must go wrong with you and me:
So much my conscience whispers in your ear,
Which none but heaven, and you, and I, shall hear.

(I.i.40–3)

The world of *King John* is thus one in which the title to the kingdom is in dispute, and the King occupies a position which he and his mother doubt, for all his seeming security, to be legally his. The second half of scene i, in which the Faulconbridge brothers are introduced, is consequently much more overtly pertinent to the first than the corresponding scene of the anonymous play. Sir Robert Faulconbridge was one of King Richard's followers, and the title to his lands, like the title to the throne, is unexpectedly obscure. In both cases it is the legality of an older man's succession which is at issue, and the trial which ensues of Philip's legitimacy is much more rigorous in its exposition of the law than the examination conducted in the earlier play:

K.John.   What men are you?
Bast[ard]. Your faithful subject I, a gentleman,
  Born in Northamptonshire, and eldest son,
  As I suppose, to Robert Faulconbridge,
  A soldier, by the honour-giving hand
  Of Coeur-de-lion knighted in the field.
K.John. What art thou?
Rob[ert]. The son and heir to that same Faulconbridge.
King J. Is that the elder, and art thou the heir?
  You came not of one mother then, it seems.
Bast. Most certain of one mother, mighty king;
  That is well known; and, as I think, one father:
  But for the certain knowledge of that truth
  I put you o'er to heaven and to my mother:
  Of that I doubt, as all men's children may.
Elea. Out on thee, rude man! thou dost shame thy mother
  And wound her honour with this diffidence.
Bast. I, madam? no, I have no reason for it;
  That is my brother's plea and none of mine;
  The which if he can prove, a pops me out
  At least from fair five hundred pound a year:
  Heaven guard my mother's honour, and my land!
K.John. A good blunt fellow. Why, being younger born,
  Doth he lay claim to thine inheritance?
Bast. I know not why – except to get the land –

But once he slander'd me with bastardy:
But whe'r I be as true begot or no,
That still I lay upon my mother's head;
But that I am as well begot, my liege –
Fair fall the bones that took the pains for me! –
Compare our faces and be judge yourself.
If old Sir Robert did beget us both
And were our father, and this son like him,
O old Sir Robert, father, on my knee
I give heaven thanks I was not like to thee!
K.John. Why, what a madcap hath heaven lent us here!
Elea. He hath a trick of Coeur-de-lion's face;
The accent of his tongue affecteth him.
Do you not read some tokens of my son
In the large composition of this man?
K.John. Mine eye hath well examined his parts
And finds them perfect Richard. Sirrah, speak,
What doth move you to claim your brother's land?
Bast. Because he hath a half-face, like my father!
With half that face would he have all my land:
A half-faced groat five hundred pound a year!
Rob. My gracious liege, when that my father liv'd,
Your brother did employ my father much –
Bast. Well sir, by this you cannot get my land:
Your tale must be how he employed my mother.
Rob. – And once dispatch'd him in an embassy
To Germany, there with the emperor
To treat of high affairs touching that time.
Th'advantage of his absence took the king
And in the mean time sojourn'd at my father's,
Where how he did prevail I shame to speak;
But truth is truth: large lengths of seas and shores
Between my father and my mother lay,
As I have heard my father speak himself,
When this same lusty gentleman was got.
Upon his death-bed he by will bequeath'd
His lands to me, and took it on his death
That this my mother's son was none of his;
And if he were, he came into the world
Full fourteen weeks before the course of time.
Then, good my liege, let me have what is mine,
My father's land, as was my father's will.

(I.i.49–115)

The case advanced here differs in two significant respects from that argued by the Robert of *The Troublesome Reign*. In the first place, where the earlier Philip's father acknowledged him and regarded him as his 'lawful heir' (Part 1, Scene i, line 121), Shakespeare's Sir Robert denied that he was the father of his wife's elder son, and excluded him from his will. This departure from the source not only serves to confirm Philip's illegitimacy, but introduces an issue of crucial importance to the King himself, the validity of wills in determining rights of inheritance. John has succeeded to the throne on the basis not of linear succession (upon which Arthur's claim depends) but on the testamentary disposition of the previous monarch — and it is the validity of that process which the French dispute. In trying Philip's case, John is thus passing judgement (at one level) on his own and the decisions that he makes are crucial in relation to the spectator's view of his position. At the same time, while heightening the insecurity of Philip's familial position, Shakespeare augments the unlikelihood that Sir Robert was in fact his father. Where the younger son of the earlier play claims that his brother was born 'six weeks before the account [his] father made' (line 167), Shakespeare's Philip came 'Full fourteen weeks before the course of time' (I.i.113), making it virtually certain that he was not fathered by his mother's husband. Where the 'proofs' offered by the anonymous playwright's Robert were patently 'frivolous', those advanced by Shakespeare's claimant clearly stand on much firmer ground, yet the judgement passed by the King is essentially the same, though much more firmly located within English law:

> K. John. Sirrah, your brother is legitimate;
>   Your father's wife did after wedlock bear him,
>   And if she did play false, the fault was hers;
>   Which fault lies on the hazards of all husbands
>   That marry wives. Tell me, how if my brother,
>   Who, as you say, took pains to get this son,
>   Had of your father claim'd this son for his?
>   In sooth, good friend, your father might have kept
>   This calf, bred from his cow, from all the world;
>   In sooth he might; then, if he were my brother's,
>   My brother might not claim him; nor your father,
>   Being none of his, refuse him: this concludes;
>   My mother's son did get your father's heir;
>   Your father's heir must have your father's land.

(I.i.116–29)

Clearly this exposition of the law is in line with the position outlined by Lord Coke (cf. 'If the husband be within the four seas [at some time during pregnancy] ... no proof is to be admitted to prove the child a bastard'). Though patently not the son of his putative father, Philip is legitimate in the eyes of the law, and though John remains silent on the issue, he gives tacit assent to the assertion that no will can overturn the right to inherit:

> Rob. Shall then my father's will be of no force
>   To dispossess that child which is not his?
> Bast. Of no more force to dispossess me, sir,
>   Than was his will to get me, as I think.

(I.i.130–3)

The strict legality of Shakespeare's trial scene, together with the much greater degree of doubt thrown on the paternity of the central figure, serves to sharpen the audience's awareness of the ambiguities of the play world. John's judgement in relation to Philip highlights the dubiety of his own position, while securing Philip's entitlement to property to which he has no claim by any tie of blood. Once his legitimacy has been established, however, Philip opts as in the earlier play for the status that his brother had sought to impose upon him, impelled not by supernatural prompting but by contempt for the cast of man that his brother represents, and the desire for self-definition. Asked by Eleanor,

> Whether hadst thou rather be a Faulconbridge,
> And like thy brother, to enjoy thy land,
> Or the reputed son of Coeur-de-lion,
> Lord of thy presence and no land beside?

he responds without hesitation,

> Bast. Madam, and if my brother had my shape,
>   And I had his, Sir Robert's his like him;
>   And if my legs were two such riding-rods,
>   My arms such eel-skins stuff'd, my face so thin
>   That in mine ear I durst not stick a rose
>   Lest men should say 'Look, where three-farthings goes!'
>   And, to his shape, were heir to all this land,
>   Would I might never stir from off this place,
>   I would give it every foot to have this face:
>   I would not be Sir Knob in any case.
> Elea. I like thee well: wilt thou forsake thy fortune,
>   Bequeath thy land to him and follow me?

I am a soldier and now bound to France.
Bast. Brother, take you my land, I'll take my chance.
     Your face hath got five hundred pound a year.
     …
King J. From henceforth bear his name whose form thou bearest:
     Kneel thou down Philip, but rise more great,
     Arise Sir Richard, and Plantagenet.
Bast. Brother by th'mother's side, give me your hand:
     My father gave me honour, yours gave land.
     Now blessed be the hour, by night or day,
     When I was got, Sir Robert was away!

(I.i.134–66)

The situation presented here is clearly the reverse of the position that conventionally obtains in the tale of the bastard son. Rather than being excluded from the community by virtue of his unnatural birth, Shakespeare's Philip is secure in his inheritance, and elects to forego a legitimacy which he sees as shameful for a bastardy which brings honour rather than disrepute. Where the bastard traditionally resents the circumstances of his birth and nurtures a hatred for those responsible for his outcast condition, the newly created 'Richard' celebrates his conception and delights in the irregularity of the union from which he comes:

Elea. I am thy grandam, Richard; call me so.
Bast. Madam, by chance but not by truth; what though?
     Something about, a little from the right,
     In at the window, or else o'er the hatch:
     Who dares not stir by day must walk by night,
     And have is have, however men do catch.
     Near or far off, well won is still well shot,
     And I am I, howe'er I was begot.

(I.i.168–75)

At the same time, however, while Philip/Richard is a bastard in legal terms by choice, and thus freed from both the opprobrium and the rancour conventionally associated with the illegitimate condition, the union from which he springs is adulterous by nature, defining him as an outsider in relation to the moral order of his world. From the moment of his first appearance his attitudes are clearly heterodox, differentiating him from both his brother and the decorum of the court. Unlike the bastard of *The Troublesome Reign* whose opening speeches are deferential and concerned with his mother's reputation (cf. Part I, Scene i, lines 87–90), Shakespeare's bastard is irreverent as Eleanor points out

(I.i.64–5), blunt rather than diplomatic in his stance towards his case. His impulsive repudiation of his land contrasts sharply with the attitudes of both John and his brother, while he exhibits a wayward sense of humour that plays insistently on sex, setting him aside from the formal gravity (and politic rationality) of the court. Many of his characteristics, moreover, serve to align him with the malign outcasts of the traditional tale. His boldness, irreverence, 'mounting spirit' (I.i.206), and quickness of mind, are all attributes conventionally associated with 'natural' sons, while his insistence upon his selfhood is archetypal, defining him as a man apart. Where Robert is concerned with paternity, and his rights as his father's son, Philip constantly harps on his own attributes, revealing a keen sense of personal worth, summed up in the assertion that

> I am I, howe'er I was begot.
>
> (I.i.175)

While having thus from one perspective elected his status, Philip consequently emerges from another as a bastard by nature, and this ambiguity is crucial to the role that he enacts in the course of the play. Shakespeare's story of the illegitimate son may be seen as an alternative one not simply because it turns on elective rather than involuntary bastardy but because it constitutes in its workings a mirror image of the conventional tale, in that the outsider is not presented as a disruptive force at war with the social group but as an unaligned individual caught up in a struggle between forces of doubtful legitimacy. John's rule, as his mother admits, is based on possession, rather than right (cf. I.i.40–3), and is supported by a will of dubious status (cf. II.i.191–3); Arthur's claim to the throne is made problematic by his dependence upon the French whose altruism is a mask for self-interest (cf. II.i. 416–560); while the influence exerted by the Pope is productive of war rather than peace (cf. III.iii.107–83) and is political rather than spiritual. In short, the succession crisis that ensues upon the death of Richard I is presented as having generated a world in which all order has broken down and in which right conduct is consequently available only to one who rejects his place in the social group, and is both physically and spiritually a 'bastard to the time' (I.i.207).

The detachment of the Bastard, in all senses of the term, affords the dramatist a vehicle for objective commentary upon the play world. Whereas the illegitimate sons of the conventional story are locked into an antagonistic response to their situation, in *King John* it is those advancing the legitimacy of their competing claims who descend into violence and vituperation, while the Bastard observes them in aloof amusement. Having been installed, for example, in his new position as Coeur-de-Lion's son, he comments with the accuracy of the disengaged observer upon the behaviour expected of (and towards one) rising in society:

> A foot of honour better than I was,
> But many a many foot of land the worse.
> Well, now can I make any Joan a lady.
> 'Good den, Sir Richard!' - 'God-a-mercy, fellow!' -
> And if his name be George, I'll call him Peter;
> For new made honour doth forget men's names:
> 'Tis too respective and too sociable
> For your conversion. Now your traveller,
> He and his toothpick at my worship's mess,
> And when my knightly stomach is suffic'd,
> Why then I suck my teeth and catechize
> My picked man of countries: 'My dear sir,' -
> Thus, leaning on mine elbow, I begin,
> 'I shall beseech you,' - that is Question now;
> And then comes Answer like an Absey book:
> 'O sir,' says Answer, 'at your best command;
> At your employment; at your service, sir:'
> 'No, sir,' says Question, 'I, sweet sir, at yours:'
> And so, ere Answer knows what Question would,
> Saving in dialogue of compliment,
> And talking of the Alps and Apennines,
> The Pyrenean and the river Po,
> It draws toward supper in conclusion so.

> (I.i.182–204)

This is not only well observed, testifying to the objectivity of the speaker, it defines a particular kind of world and exhibits an attitude towards it. The fact that the Bastard comments that 'new made honour doth forget men's names' implies the breakdown of a community, while evoking an alternative society of mutual recognition and respect. Similarly, the conversation that he mimics in which the communication of ideas has given place to empty compliment implies through its absurdity the existence of more meaningful modes of human interaction. Though he claims that the society he describes 'fits a mounting spirit like myself' (I.i.206) his tone registers his lack of affinity with the world that he has entered, and this disengagement, and consequent clarity of perception, is yet more evident in the following act in the scene before

Angiers. The French and English forces having failed to oblige the
townspeople to arbitrate between the claims of John and Arthur, the
opposing armies are poised to mount a joint assault upon the town
when a marriage is proposed between Blanche (John's neice) and the
Dauphin as means of reconciling the warring princes. Arthur's claim to
the English throne, the ostensible cause of the conflict, is consequently
brushed aside and a league of amity concluded that the Bastard recognizes to be motivated solely by self-interest:

> Mad world! mad kings! mad composition!
> John, to stop Arthur's title in the whole,
> Hath willingly departed with a part:
> And France, whose armour conscience buckled on,
> Whom zeal and charity brought to the field
> As God's own soldier, rounded in the ear
> With that same purpose-changer, that sly divel,
> That broker, that still breaks the pate of faith,
> That daily break-vow, he that wins of all,
> Of kings, of beggars, old men, young men, maids,
> Who, having no external thing to lose
> But the word 'maid', cheats the poor maid of that,
> That smooth-fac'd gentleman, tickling commodity,
> Commodity, the bias of the world,
> The world, who of itself is peised well,
> Made to run even upon even ground,
> Till this advantage, this vile drawing bias,
> This sway of motion, this commodity,
> Makes it take head from all indifferency,
> From all direction, purpose, course, intent:
> And this same bias, this commodity,
> This bawd, this broker, this all-changing word,
> Clapp'd on the outward eye of fickle France,
> Hath drawn him from his own determin'd aid,
> From a resolv'd and honourable war,
> To a most base and vile-concluded peace.

> (II.i.561–86)

While the mocking clear-sightedness he exhibits here aligns him with
the outsiders of the traditional tale, his attitudes are the reverse of those
conventionally displayed by illegitimate sons. Rather than feeling his
worth to be impugned by a system from which he is excluded, he sees
legitimate society as self-seeking, 'base', and morally insane, while he
himself is sympathetic to the victims of self-interest. While those around

him are dedicated to the pursuit of personal gain, he regards their activities as dishonourable and 'vile', a distortion of the cosmic order, drawing the well-peised world from its appointed path.

The process of reversal at work here is evident in the Bastard's conduct in the course of the play. In the inverted world that the drama sets up it is the legitimate members of society who perpetrate savage and unnatural acts, and the Bastard who upholds the natural order. Filial piety, for example, has been transferred here from the legitimate to the illegitimate son. While Robert seeks to brand his mother an adulteress before the court, Philip declines to pursue the truth regarding the circumstances of his conception until he and Lady Faulconbridge are alone (cf. I.i.220ff.). Where the illegitimate son of the conventional tale is hostile towards those responsible for his outcast condition, Philip is proud of his lineage, and fights for the lion skin that once belonged to Coeur-de-Lion. The sense of kinship he exhibits here is in stark contrast to the attitudes of the legitimate members of the royal family. John makes war upon his nephew and is supported throughout by Eleanor, the grandmother of the child; Constance and Eleanor (mother-in-law and daughter-in-law) view one another as 'monstrous' (II.i.173–4); while the Dauphin invades a kingdom governed by the uncle of his wife. Whereas in Sidney's *Arcadia* it is the bastard Plexirtus who is responsible for his father's blinding, in *King John* it is the King who orders his nephew's eyes to be put out, and the Bastard who deplores the death of the boy as 'a damned and a bloody work' (IV.iii.57). While the nobles transfer their allegiances from John to the Dauphin and back to John again, the Bastard struggles to sustain the unity of the kingdom, and remains loyal to his failing kinsman. As pacts and words are broken around him in the pursuit of private gain, it is he who acts as the agent for the resumption of 'lineal state' (V.vii.102) and for a return to a natural order in which the 'stars [i.e. peers] … move in [their] right spheres' (V.vii.74).

The inversion of the paradigmatic relationship between the Bastard and his world clearly serves in *King John* as an implicit criticism of the society in which the action takes place. The pervasive degeneracy and escalating disorder is accentuated by the implication that a norm has been perverted, and that right conduct is available only to one outside a debased and increasingly anarchic social group. In this context, the figure of the bastard functions not as a diabolic force to be resisted in order that humane values may be restored, but as a species of yardstick by which the degeneration of the play world may be measured, and as an objective commentator upon corrupt institutions. Just as Hal in *1 Henry IV* elects to be a prodigal in order to disengage himself from his father's court, so Philip elects his superficially disreputable status and in doing so opts, paradoxically, out of rather than into a depraved state. Where Hal's conduct, however, is at one with the mores of his society, and contributes to the exploration of power politics that takes place in the course of the play, the stance adopted by the Bastard is essentially a critical one, functioning as an indictment (rather than an extension) of the national condition. Instead of inviting audience complicity in the exploitation of those less clear-sighted than himself, he guides the spectator towards an assessment of the values in force in the world of the play, distancing them from the protagonists. It is this objectivity – the judgemental stance that he encourages the audience to adopt – that gives Shakespeare's alternative tale of the bastard son a particular interest for those concerned with dramatic censorship, and political comment on the Renaissance stage.

First performed in the mid-1590s, *King John* was written during a period of considerable political uncertainty. Though Elizabeth herself refused to acknowledge the fact, her life was drawing to a close and as an unmarried monarch she had failed to provide her realm with the requisite heir. Long and successful though her reign had been, moreover, her entitlement to rule was far from clear cut. Not only was her legitimacy disputed by the Catholic community who denied the legality of Henry VIII's initial divorce,[21] but she had been formally bastardized in the 1536 second Act of Succession, and only implicitly reinstated. At the same time, the position was complicated by the provisions of Henry VIII's will in which he directed that the throne should pass to the descendants of his younger sister Mary (as opposed to his elder sister, Margaret) should his line fail. To many of his subjects, of his three children only Mary (as the issue of his first marriage) had any right to the throne, while his decision to debar the offspring of his elder sister was without legal force. Elizabeth herself, in order to protect her own position, had been driven to order the execution of her cousin Mary Queen of Scots, to some the rightful heir to the throne but excluded by Henry's will. In short, a number of parallels existed between the

---

succession crises of the thirteenth and the sixteenth centuries, and these were not lost on writers seeking to advance the causes of a variety of claimants to the throne.[22] Moreover, from the time of Bale's *King Johan* (1538) John had been presented on the English stage as a precursor of Henry VIII in his dealings with the Pope, and had been depicted in that light circa 1588 in *The Troublesome Reign*. In short, a late sixteenth-century audience would have been alive to resonances of the Shakespearian drama that are lost to us today, and would have been ready to make connections between the politics of their own period and events on the stage.

The History play was the dominant dramatic form of the Elizabethan period and conventionally focused on the rights and responsibilities of kingship and the intimate relationship between the moral health of the monarch and the well-being of the subject. Set in the courts of classical Greece (cf. Lyly's *Campaspe*, 1580–4), Scotland (cf. Greene's *James IV*, c.1590–1), or mediaeval England (cf. the anonymous *Edward III*, c.1593–4?), and thus ostensibly remote from the Elizabethan world, the plays reflected upon issues pertinent to their own time while seeking to evade the hostile attentions of the censor.[23] Evidence of the nature of dramatic censorship in the 1590s is supplied by the mutilated play texts that have come down to us, most notably *The Book of Sir Thomas More* (1592–3?) (in which Shakespeare may have had a hand)[24] in which entire scenes and long passages of dialogue have been marked for dele-tion. Two areas of the play in particular attracted the notice of the authorities – those relating to More's opposition to Henry VIII's breach with Rome, and those dealing with public hostility to the immigrant community – a phenomenon common to both early and late sixteenth-century London. Both areas of sensitivity have relevance to Shakespeare's *King John*. While on the one hand, the play is politically unexceptionable in that it is critical of the power of the papacy, and emphasizes the importance of national unity, on the other it deals with

22. See Braunmuller, (ed.) *King John*, p. 59.
23. For a full discussion of censorship on the Renaissance stage see Janet Clare (1990) *'Art Made Tongue-tied by Authority': Elizabethan and Jacobean Dramatic Censorship*, Manchester University Press.
24. For a seminal discussion of the authorship of the play see R.C. Bald (1949) *'The Booke of Sir Thomas More* and its Problems', *Shakespeare Survey 2*, Cambridge University Press, pp. 44–61. The hands at work in the drama have been explored more recently in Vittorio Gabrieli and Giorgio Melchiori (eds) (1990) *Sir Thomas More*, Revels Plays, Manchester University Press.

an issue of major contemporary relevance, the problems ensuing upon the breakdown of linear succession. Though not an allegory, in that no precise correspondance is set up between the events of the thirteenth and sixteenth centuries, and there is no overt invitation to identify Elizabethan personages under Plantagenet guises, the drama nevertheless plays out the implications of the contemporary situation, investigating the kind of world that ensues on the breakdown of the right to rule, a world in which no authority is indisputably legitimate.

Whereas it was once assumed that Shakespearian drama upholds the divine right of kings and that the chronicle histories chart the emergence of sanctified monarchy under the Tudors, recent criticism (as noted in Chapter 1) has read the plays in much less politically orthodox ways. *King John* is an important work in this respect in that it is at once a damning exposure of the processes of political legitimization and a markedly undeferential work. While John and the French King, for example, justify their own conduct by defining the other's power as 'usurped' (cf. II.i.112–121), calling on law and religion in support of their positions (cf. II.i.299), the Bastard's ironic commentary on their actions demystifies the language of power politics, and exposes both the pragmatism and ultimate absurdity (cf. II.i.561–98) beneath the ceremony of state. Though overtly concerned with events at a considerable historical distance from the political actualities of the 1590s, the play presents nevertheless an uncompromising picture of the spiritual dereliction of a society in which self-interest rather than probity lies at the heart of the national life, and its contemporary relevance would not have been lost upon an audience familiar with the analogy between the reigns of John and Henry VIII, and alive to the dangers of the gathering succession crisis. Rather than being a History play in the modern sense of the term (i.e. a drama evoking the actuality of a past age) *King John* may thus be regarded as a much more politically engaged work. Harnessing a web of traditional assumptions regarding legitimacy to a commonplace historical parallel, it sets up a deflatory interaction between event and choric commentary, instigating a critique of a society in which the moral fabric has been eroded that is applicable to more than one time. Shakespeare's alternative tale of the bastard son, in short, while located within a literary tradition and avoiding direct contemporary reference, lends itself to analysis as a politically charged and potentially dangerous work. By presenting a mirror image of the conventional story of the malign outsider pitted against the social group the dramatist reflects, not upon the depravity of the individual and the dangerous potency of diabolic agencies, but on the dubious process of legitimation and the spiritual debasement of an age. Though aligned with the forces of order, and an outsider in legal terms by choice, the bastard who rallies the English against the French and oversees the lawful succession of Henry III may thus be regarded, paradoxically, as every bit as subversive in his attitudes as his more overtly heterodox literary brethren engaged in plotting a brother's downfall or plucking out a father's eyes.

Chapter 3

A Midsummer Night's Dream and the Tale of the Faithful Friends

There was in the city of Rome a noble senator named Fulvius, who sent his son called Titus, being a child, to the city of Athens … there to learn good letters, and caused him to be hosted with a worshipful man of that city called Chremes. This Chremes happened to have also a son named Gisippus, who not only was equal to the said young Titus in years, but also in stature, proportion of body, favour and colour of visage, countenance and speech. The two children were so alike that without much difficulty it could not be discerned of their proper [i.e. own] parents which was Titus from Gisippus or Gisippus from Titus. These two young gentlemen, as they seemed to be one in form and personage, so shortly after acquaintance the same nature wrought in their hearts such a mutual affection that their wills and appetites daily more and more so confederated themselves that it seemed none other when their names were declared but that they had only changed their places … They together and at one time went to their learning and study, at one time to their meals and refection; they delighted both in one doctrine and profited equally therein … At the last died Chremes, which was not only to his son, but also to Titus, cause of much sorrow and heaviness. Gisippus, by the goods of his father, was known to be a man of great substance … and he then being of ripe years … his friends, kin and allies exhorted him busily to take a wife, to the intent he might increase his lineage and progeny. But the young man, having his heart already wedded to his friend Titus, and his mind fixed to the study of philosophy, fearing that marriage should be the occasion to sever him both from the one and the other, refused of long time to be persuaded, until at the last, partly by the importunate calling on of his kinsmen, partly by the consent and advice of his dear friend Titus, thereto by other desired, he assented to marry such one as should like him … His friends found a young gentlewoman, which in equality of years, virtuous conditions, nobility of blood, beauty and sufficient riches they thought was for such a young man apt and convenient. And when they and her friends upon the covenants of marriage were thoroughly accorded, they counselled Gisippus to repair unto the maiden, and to behold how her person contented him. And he so doing found her in every form and condition according to his expectation and appetite, whereat he much rejoiced and became of her amorous, in so much as many and often times he, leaving Titus at his study, secretly repaired unto her. Notwithstanding, the fervent love that he had to his friend Titus at the last surmounted shamefastness, wherefore he disclosed to him his secret journeys, and what delectation he took in beholding the excellent beauty of her whom he purposed to marry ... And on a time he having with him his friend Titus went to his lady, of whom he was received most joyously, but Titus ... as he beheld so heavenly a personage ... was thereat abashed, and had the heart through pierced with the fiery dart of blind Cupid. Of the which wound the anguish was so exceeding and vehement, that neither the study of philosophy, neither the remembrance of his dear friend Gisippus, who so much loved and trusted him, could anything withdraw him from that unkind appetite ... At the last, the pain became so intolerable ... he was enforced to keep his bed ... brought in such feebleness that his legs might not sustain his body. Gisippus, missing his dear friend Titus, was much abashed, and hearing that he lay sick in his bed, had forthwith his heart pierced with heaviness, and with all speed came to him where he lay ... and with a comfortable countenance demanded of Titus what was the cause of his disease ... conjur[ing] him that for the fervent and entire love that had been, and yet was, between them, he would no longer hide from him his grief, and that there was nothing to him so dear or precious ... that might restore Titus to health, but that he should gladly and without grudging employ it ... Titus, constrained, all blushing and ashamed, holding down his head, brought forth with great difficulty his words in this wise, 'My dear and most loving friend, withdraw your friendly offers, cease of your courtesy ... take rather your knife and slay me here where I lie ... Alas, why forgot ye that our minds and appetites were ever one, and that also what so ye liked was ever to me in like degree pleasant? ... Gisippus, I say your trust is the cause that I am entrapped. The rays or beams issuing from the eyes of her whom ye have chosen ... have thrilled throughout the middle of my heart, and in such wise burneth it that above all things I desire to be out of this wretched and most unkind life, which is not worthy the company of so noble and loving a friend as ye be.' And therewith Titus concluded his confession with so profound and bitter a sigh ... that it seemed that all his body should be dissolved ... into salt drops. But Gisippus, as he were therewith nothing astonished or discontented, with an assured countenance and merry regard, embracing Titus and kissing him, answered in this wise, 'Why Titus, is this your only sickness and grief that ye so uncourteously have so long concealed? ... I knowledge my folly ... that in showing to you her whom I loved I remembered not the common estate of our nature, nor the agreeableness or (as I might say) the unity of our two appetites ... Wherefore it is only I that have offended ... Think ye me such a fool or ignorant person that I know not the power of Venus where she listeth to show her importable violence? Have not ye well resisted against such a goddess, that for my sake ye have striven with her almost to the death? What more loyalty or truth can I require of you? ... I confess to you, Titus, I love that maiden as much as any wise man might ... but now I perceive that the affection of love toward her surmounteth in you above measure ... Therefore, gentle friend Titus, dismay you not at the chance of love, but receive it joyously with me, that am with you nothing discontented ... Here I renounce to you clearly all my title and interest that I now have or might have in that fair maiden. ... I force not what pain that I abide, so that ye, my friend Titus, may be safe and pleasantly enjoy your desires, to the increasing of your felicity.

(Sir Thomas Elyot, *The Boke Named The Governour*, 1531)[1]

The story of Titus and Gisippus, designed to illustrate 'the figure of perfect amity' was well known in the sixteenth century, and formed one strand of the complex web of friendship literature popular throughout the Renaissance and Middle Ages. The exemplary devotion exhibited by Gisippus in yielding up his mistress is later reciprocated by Titus who places his life in jeopardy by confessing to a murder he has not committed when his friend is (wrongly) accused of the crime. The story, which is derived by Elyot from Boccaccio,[2] occurs in a variety of literary forms, both verse and dramatic versions (e.g. by William Walters and by Ralph Radcliffe) being recorded in the sixteenth century.[3] The two strands of the tale, the tension between love and friendship, and the friends' willingness to sacrifice their lives for one another, also occur in isolation in other versions of the story. In Chaucer's *The Knight's Tale*,[4] for example, which looks back to Boccaccio's *La Teseide*, the two friends (who are also cousins) fall in love with the same woman but do not face the obligation to surrender their lives for one another, while the eponymous heroes of Richard Edwards' *Damon and Pithias* (1565), a play written for performance by boys, are not tested in the amatory arena, but pledge life and liberty on one another's behalf.

1. The passage quoted (from Book II, Chapter XII) is based upon the text in Geoffrey Bullough (1957–75) *Narrative and Dramatic Sources of Shakespeare* vol. i, Routledge and Kegan Paul, pp. 212–17. Spelling and punctuation, however, have been modernized.
2. See *The Decameron*, Day 10, Story 8.
3. The tale is also alluded to in other literary works, e.g. Spenser's *The Faerie Queene* (Book IV, Canto X, Stanzas 26–7).
4. Dramatized by (among others) Shakespeare and Fletcher in *The Two Noble Kinsmen* (1613).

Though fundamentally didactic in impulse, the tale does not always conform in its various redactions to the exemplary process enacted in the version that Elyot relates. Palamon and Arcite, for example, in Chaucer's *The Knight's Tale*, having fallen in love with the same woman, do not seek to subdue their amatory feelings in the interests of friendship, but engage in a life-long struggle over Emily that ends only when Arcite, having triumphed in combat and then been thrown from his horse, renounces his prospective bride to his cousin on his death bed. Rather than exhibiting the superiority of masculine friendship to heterosexual love, this version of the tale is concerned with the consuming nature of passion and the values of the chivalric code, the courtesy with which the two knights arm one another before their first combat exhibiting not merely their friendship, but knightly virtue. Other friends are less honourable in their pursuit of a mistress. While Palamon and Arcite are open with one another in their competition for Emily, the eponymous hero of Lyly's *Euphues: The Anatomy of Wit* (1578) not only deceives his friend Philautus about his passion for the other's mistress but makes their amity a means of gaining access to her presence, through the pretence of loving one of her friends. In this case, the relationship between the three central figures demonstrates, not an ideal of conduct sustained in the face of extreme circumstance, but the infirm basis of the relationship between the friends, the moral failure of Euphues, and the fickleness of the lady he attempts to win. It is this version of the story that Shakespeare takes up in *The Two Gentlemen of Verona* (c.1593), his first play on the love and friendship theme. Once again faithful friends fall in love with the same lady, but Proteus, unlike Titus, deceives and betrays the man who relies upon his faith, though Valentine, like Gisippus (but unlike Lyly's Philautus) unhesitatingly renounces his mistress in favour of his friend.

Whether presenting types or anti-types, the versions of the inherited story outlined above have much in common. In every instance the ideal that is upheld or betrayed is that of masculine friendship, while in the majority of redactions the stress that is placed upon the relationship springs from the sexual impulse. The young men at the centre of the story are lifelong friends and the likeness between them is constantly stressed. Thus just as Titus and Gisippus are similar in appearance, have had the same upbringing and have been inseparable from boyhood, so Palamon and Arcite are cousins, united by blood and their upbringing in Thebes, have fought together in battle, and endured long years of imprisonment together. Similarly, Euphues chooses Philautus as his friend because of the likeness between them both in station and habit of mind, seeing in him 'the lively image'[5] of his own person. At the same time considerable stress is laid by many of the tales on the importance of education in determining right conduct and cementing the bond between honourable minds. Titus is sent to Athens to learn 'good letters' in the house of Chremes, studies philosophy with Gisippus, and profits (as his friend does) from his studies. Conversely, Euphues' upbringing is censured on his arrival in Naples by the fatherly Eubulus, and his lack of moral understanding is reflected in his behaviour towards Philautus. In *The Two Gentlemen of Verona*, Valentine leaves Verona in order to expand his understanding of the world, while Proteus' father and uncle are anxious that he too should expand his horizons, cf:

> Ant[onio]. Tell me, Panthino, what sad talk was that
> Wherewith my brother held you in the cloister?
> Pan[thino]. 'Twas of his nephew Proteus, your son.
> Ant. Why, what of him?
> Pan.   He wonder'd that your lordship
> Would suffer him to spend his youth at home,
> While other men, of slender reputation,
> Put forth their sons, to seek preferment out:
> Some to the wars, to try their fortune there;
> Some, to discover islands far away;
> Some, to the studious universities.
> For any, or for all these exercises,
> He said that Proteus your son was meet,
> And did request me to importune you
> To let him spend his time no more at home.
> ...
> Ant. Nor need'st thou much importune me to that
> Whereon this month I have been hammering.
> I have consider'd well his loss of time,
> And how he cannot be a perfect man,
> Not being tried and tutor'd in the world.
> ...
> Then tell me, whither were I best to send him?
> Pan. I think your lordship is not ignorant
> How his companion, youthful Valentine,
> Attends the Emperor in his royal court.

5. Quoted from Morris William Croll and Harry Clemons (eds) (1964, first published 1916) *Euphues, The Anatomy of Wit: Euphues and his England*, Russell and Russell, p. 29.

...
Twere good, I think, your lordship sent him thither:
There shall he practise tilts and tournaments,
Hear sweet discourse, converse with noblemen,
And be in eye of every exercise
Worthy his youth and nobleness of birth.

                                                          (I.iii.1–33)

While the mental gifts of the protagonists are emphasized, physical
prowess (evoked here in Panthino's reference to tilts and tournaments)
also plays an important part in the majority of love and friendship tales.
Chaucer's heroes are knights, who are first discovered lying together on
the battlefield, and they engage in two formal combats for Emily in
which the rules of chivalry are strictly observed; Euphues and Philautus
threaten violence on one another, but their failure to match their words
with heroic action is evidence of the moral emptiness which is the
source of their eventual failure; while Valentine confronts Proteus on
discovering him attempting to rape Sylvia, and subsequently outfaces a
second rival (Thurio) in the presence of the Duke.

The ideals embodied in the situations presented in these stories are
firmly related to concepts of gentlemanliness in both mediaeval (i.e.
chivalric) and later Renaissance senses. Elyot's tale presents an ideal of
human behaviour which is the product of birth and education, in which
friendship takes precedence over baser emotions, the self is subordinated
to the happiness of others, loyalty is a primary virtue, and the capacity
for self-sacrifice the index of the noble mind. In its sixteenth-century
versions, the story clearly offers a model for behaviour designed to con-
tribute to the humanist goal – the improvement of the individual and
the creation of a more civilized (in the fullest sense of that term) society.
The Boke Named the Governour belongs to a tradition of literary works
that includes Castiglione's *The Courtier* (1528), and Spenser's *The Faerie
Queene* (1590–6) in which all the qualifications of the ideal noblemen,
ethical, intellectual, military and courtly are laid down as models for
those seeking to perfect themselves in the gentlemanly virtues, and thus
become fit servants of both their earthly and divine masters. The sacrifices of Gisippus for Titus and Titus for Gisippus, for all the fancifulness
of the context in which the actions take place, are thus serious exempli-
fications of courses of conduct that work towards the creation of a
moral order, while the acts of betrayal committed by Euphues and
Proteus exhibit a progress towards the bestial and away from the divine,
signalled by Proteus' physical onslaught upon Sylvia, and Lucilla's

preference for the degenerate Curio as against the more accomplished Euphues and Philautus.

The rejection of the lower passions in favour of reason, and of sexual love in place of asexual comradeship locates these works in a highly abstract, intellectual arena that in itself is traditionally masculine. The completion of the expected pattern (i.e. the triumph of friendship over passion or the given word over fear of death) is evocative of an orderly universe in which man, God's prime creation and microcosm of the state, conforms to a hierarchical functioning in which wit triumphs over will, self-discipline over contingency. Though modern audiences find Valentine's renunciation of his mistress to Proteus hard to accept at the close of *The Two Gentlemen of Verona*, his action conforms to a tradition that aligns him with the workings of a harmonious universe, while Proteus' act of betrayal is defined in terms that register the dislocation that a breach of trust between friends effects in a wider sphere:

> Treacherous man,
> Thou hast beguil'd my hopes; nought but mine eye
> Could have persuaded me: now I dare not say
> I have one friend alive; thou wouldst disprove me.
> Who should be trusted now, when one's right hand
> Is perjured to the bosom? Proteus,
> I am sorry I must never trust thee more,
> But count the world a stranger for thy sake.
>
> (V.iv.63–70)

Friendships are common in Shakespearian drama, but only two plays (*The Two Gentlemen of Verona* and *Two Noble Kinsmen*) involve competition between youthful comrades for a mistress, while a third, *The Winter's Tale* (c.1610–11) turns on the sexual jealousy that erupts between friends of mature years after their separation and marriage. Nevertheless, these are not the only items in the corpus which exhibit the influence of the love and friendship tradition. Benedick in *Much Ado About Nothing* (1598), for example, is obliged to choose between his love for Beatrice and his friendship for Claudio, while Antonio and Portia in *The Merchant of Venice* (1596–8) exert competing claims upon the loyalty of Bassanio. Less obviously, *A Midsummer Night's Dream* also looks back to the tissue of ideas exemplified by the tale of Titus and Gisippus, but in this instance the relationship with the inherited story is more complex in that its terms are largely reversed.

Though Chaucer's *The Knight's Tale* forms one of the principal sources of *A Midsummer Night's Dream*, supplying the frame plot of the marriage between Theseus and Hippolyta, at first sight the story which the borrowed material enfolds bears little resemblance to the tale of Palamon and Arcite. Shakespeare's play concerns the cross-affections of a pair of young lovers, their nocturnal experiences in a wood outside Athens, their manipulation by supernatural beings, and final concord in marriage. Nevertheless, the sexual competition that lies at the heart of Chaucer's story does find its way into the play. Lysander and Demetrius compete for the hand of Hermia, and both having abandoned her, fight for Helena in the wood, while Lysander echoes the traditional offer of renunciation when he suggests that he yield to Demetrius the lady whom he no longer loves:

> You love Hermia; this you know I know:
> And here, with all good will, with all my heart,
> In Hermia's love I yield you up my part.

(III.ii.163–5)

The lines are evocative of Valentine's surrender of Sylvia to Proteus in *The Two Gentlemen of Verona* which themselves look back to the strand of the love and friendship story exemplified by the history of Titus and Gisippus, but there is no suggestion in *A Midsummer Night's Dream* that Lysander and Demetrius were once inseparable companions. Though they are clearly well known to one another (Lysander is aware, for example, of Demetrius' courtship and desertion of Helena; cf. I.i.106–110), neither experiences any tension between loyalty to a friend and a consuming heterosexual passion. It is in the experience of Hermia and Helena that these aspects of the tale are found, with Shakespeare inverting the conventional story by making his tale one of female friendship.

Just as Palamon and Arcite have grown up together in Thebes and Titus and Gisippus have shared their boyhood and education, so Helena and Hermia are presented as having been inseparable in youth. Reproaching Hermia for her behaviour towards her, Helena paints a vivid picture of their childhood and the strength of the bond that once existed between them:

> Is all the counsel that we two have shar'd,
> The sisters' vows, the hours that we have spent
> When we have chid the hasty-footed time
> For parting us – O, is all forgot?
> All school-days' friendship, childhood innocence?

We, Hermia, like two artificial gods,
Have with our needles created both one flower,
Both on one sampler, sitting on one cushion,
Both warbling of one song, both in one key,
As if our hands, our sides, voices and minds,
Had been incorporate. So we grew together,
Like to a double cherry, seeming parted,
But yet an union in partition,
Two lovely berries moulded on one stem;
So, with two seeming bodies, but one heart;
Two of the first, like coats in heraldry,
Due but to one and crowned with one crest.

(III.ii.198–214)

Humorous as it is, this description has much in common with Elyot's account of the youth of Titus and Gisippus, but that the occupations described are appropriate to the sex of the friends. Just as 'the same nature wrought in the hearts' of Elyot's heroes 'such a mutual affection that their wills and appetites daily more and more … confederated themselves', so Helena and Hermia 'grew together', as if their 'sides, voices and minds, / Had been incorporate'. Similarly, while 'it seemed none other when [Titus' and Gisippus'] names were declared but that they had only changed their places', Hermia and Helena 'grew together, / Like to a double cherry, seeming parted, / But yet an union in partition'. Like the male friends of the traditional story, who 'together and at one time went to their learning and study, at one time to their meals and refection … delighted both in one doctrine and profited equally therein', the two girls 'Have with [their] needles created both one flower, / Both on one sampler, sitting on one cushion, / Both warbling of one song, both in one key'. The values of a male friendship are also implicit in the imagery that Helena uses to define their former relationship. The chivalric world of Arcite and Palamon is evoked in the description of the girls as 'two of the first, like coats in heraldry, / Due but to one, and crowned with one crest', while the approximation to the divine achieved through the relationship is suggested through the capacity to create (cf. 'We, Hermia, like two artificial gods, / Have with our needles created both one flower').

Though Helena's speech is rendered ludicrous in context by Hermia's failure to understand the cause of her reproach, the friendship between the two women is not contested. Hermia agrees to meet Lysander at a place where she and Helena 'Upon faint primrose beds were wont to lie, / Emptying our bosoms of their counsel sweet' (I.i.215–6) while she refers to the other woman as her 'sweet playfellow' (I.i.220). The bond between the two is evinced by the fact that, like her male counterparts in the inherited story, Hermia places implicit trust in Helena's loyalty, confiding to her the secret of her flight from Athens with Lysander, confident that she can rely on the other's prayers for her success (I.i.220). As in the traditional story, moreover, the division between the confidantes is a product of sexual passion. While Demetrius and Lysander enact one strand of the expected pattern of action in that they pursue the same woman, Helena replicates the conventional tension between love and loyalty when her former lover, Demetrius, falls in love with her friend. Having been made the repository, like Titus and Proteus, of the confidences of a bosom companion, Helena resolves like the latter to betray friendship in the cause of love:

> How happy some o'er other some can be!
> Through Athens I am thought as fair as she.
> But what of that? Demetrius thinks not so;
> He will not know what all but he do know;
> And as he errs, doting on Hermia's eyes,
> So I, admiring of his qualities.
> …
> For, ere Demetrius look'd on Hermia's eyne,
> He hail'd down oaths that he was only mine;
> And when this hail some heat from Hermia felt,
> So he dissolv'd and show'rs of oaths did melt.
> I will go tell him of fair Hermia's flight:
> Then to the wood will he, tomorrow night,
> Pursue her; and for this intelligence
> If I have thanks, it is a dear expense.
> But herein mean I to enrich my pain,
> To have his sight thither and back again.
>
> (I.ii.226–51)

Having broken faith with Hermia, Helena comes to believe that Hermia, in turn, has betrayed her by making common cause with Lysander and Demetrius. Finding herself unexpectedly wooed in apparent mockery by both men, their avowals censured in seeming complicity by Hermia, she responds with an outraged appeal to their former friendship (quoted above), reproving her for her violation of amity, and for her breach of the solidarity expected between those of the same gender:

Will you rent our ancient love asunder
To join with men in scorning your poor friend?
It is not friendly, 'tis not maidenly;
Our sex, as well as I, may chide you for it,
Though I alone do feel the injury.

(III.ii.215–19)

The values evoked here are those that conventionally obtain in the male arena. Friendship between members of the same sex is presented as a pre-eminent relationship, while to align oneself with a lover against a bosom companion is seen as a betrayal with universal implications.

The physical conflict between those who were once comrades in arms also finds its way into the Shakespearian play. Just as Palamon and Arcite fight two heroic battles over Emily, so the rupture between Helena and Hermia leads to combat in the forest. Driven to the conclusion that Helena has stolen Lysander from her, Hermia comes to see her former friend as a 'juggler' and a 'thief of love' (III.ii.282–3), and first insults and then attempts to strike her (III.ii.303). Though Helena attests to the other's physical prowess, cf:

O, when she is angry, she is keen and shrewd;
She was a vixen when she went to school,
And though she be but little, she is fierce;

(III.ii.323–5)

she herself lacks the spirit to meet her antagonist in equal fight (cf. the martial deficiencies of other unfaithful friends) and first appeals to Lysander and Demetrius for protection:

Let her not hurt me. I was never curst;
I have no gift at all in shrewishness;

(III.ii.300–1)

and then, on finding herself alone with her opponent, abruptly vacates the field:

I will not trust you, I,
Nor longer stay in your curst company.
Your hands than mine are quicker for a fray:
My legs are longer though, to run away.

(III.ii.340–3)

On one level Shakespeare's alternative version of the conventional story is clearly productive of humour. The rituals of formal challenge, and chivalric contest, for example, are reduced to farce when the stereo-typical roles of the protagonists are reversed. Male dignity is undermined by the lover becoming the prize of female competition, while heroic combat becomes ludicrous when the battle strategies adopted are typically female rather than male (cf. 'my nails can reach unto thine eyes', III.ii.298). Similarly, the early indications of nobility afforded by the display of courage in infancy are undercut when converted into 'she was a vixen when she went to school'. While adding to the humour of the drama, however, the inversion that Shakespeare effects in the conventional stances of the dramatis personae also contributes to a much wider process of reversal at work in the world of the play. The relationships of Helena, Hermia, Demetrius and Lysander are not idiosyncratic but symptomatic, characteristic of the topsy-turvy, dream-like quality that distinguishes the drama as a whole.

Though it appears at first sight that the Athenian world of *A Midsummer Night's Dream* is governed by Theseus, it quickly becomes apparent that the larger universe in which human beings act out their parts is subject to the influence of much more powerful forces. Titania's refusal to yield to Oberon the Indian boy reared by her on the death of his mother is productive not only of dissention within the fairy kingdom, but of a wider confusion within the natural world that has repercussions in the human sphere. At odds with one another, the play's supernatural beings have dislocated the natural order, their 'brawls' (II.i.87) initiating a cosmic abrogation or reversal of roles:

> The winds, piping to us in vain,
> … have suck'd up from the sea
> Contagious fogs; which, falling in the land,
> Hath every pelting river made so proud
> That they have overborne their continents.
> The ox hath therefore stretch'd his yoke in vain,
> The ploughman lost his sweat, and the green corn
> Hath rotted ere his youth attain'd a beard;
> …
> The human mortals want their winter cheer:
> No night is now with hymn or carol blest.
> Therefore the moon, the governess of floods,
> Pale in her anger, washes all the air,
> That rheumatic diseases do abound.
> And thorough this distemperature we see
> The seasons alter: hoary-headed frosts
> Fall in the fresh lap of the crimson rose;

And on old Hiems' thin and icy crown,
An odorous chaplet of sweet summer buds
Is, as in mockery, set; the spring, the summer,
The childing autumn, angry winter, change
Their wonted liveries; and the mazed world,
By their increase, now knows not which is which.

(II.i.88–114)

The events enacted in the course of the play bear witness to this disorder. Much of the action takes place at night, when shapes are difficult to distinguish, and purposes easy to mistake (cf. 'In the night, imagining some fear,/ How easy is a bush suppos'd a bear', V.i.21–2). The moon, associated with flux, governs the drama (cf. I.i.3–4), while confusion manifests itself in both physical and emotional spheres. Bottom becomes half-man, half-beast, loses his human companions and is waited upon by supernatural beings, while Titania embraces a mortal crowned with an ass's head. The king of the fairies causes his queen to become enamoured of some 'vile thing' (II.ii.33), while human lovers abuse those to whom they have pledged their faith, and chase a spirit helter-skelter through the forest in the belief that they are following one another. The conventions of courtship are both inverted and grossly violated, while the process of pairing is oddly distorted. Helena, pursuing Demetrius, is conscious that women 'should be woo'd, and were not made to woo' (II.i.242), but is aware that in their case 'the story' has been 'chang'd' (II.i.230) and that in their world:

Apollo flies, and Daphne holds the chase;
The dove pursues the griffin, the mild hind
Makes speed to catch the tiger.

(II.i.231–3)

Demetrius, who once 'made love to Nedar's daughter' (I.i.107), threatens her with violence in the forest and abandons her to 'the mercy of wild beasts' (II.i.228), while Helena, whom he once courted, pleads to be treated as his dog:

I am your spaniel; and, Demetrius,
The more you beat me, I will fawn on you.
Use me but as your spaniel, spurn me, strike me,
Neglect me, lose me; only give me leave,
Unworthy as I am, to follow you.
What worser place can I beg in your love –

And yet a place of high respect with me –
Than to be used as you use your dog?

(II.i.203–10)

Men run from women (cf. II.i.227) while, rather than pairing, young lovers compete for affection in groups of three. Hermia is pursued by Demetrius and Lysander, who then reverse their affections, and quarrel over Helena. 'Fair Hermia' (I.i.117) becomes an 'Ethiope' (III.ii.257), a 'tawny Tartar' (III.ii.263) in the eyes of her lover, who repudiates her as a beast:

Hang off, thou cat, thou burr! Vile thing, let loose,
Or I will shake thee from me like a serpent,

(III.ii.260–1)

while Helena assumes a divine form for Demetrius (III.ii.137) who had previously declared himself sickened by her very presence (II.i.212).

The transposition of roles that Shakespeare effects in his treatment of the love and friendship story is thus consonant with other motifs of the drama, and so too is the element of the grotesque to which the handling of the inherited story gives rise. In the period that is evoked prior to the opening of the drama, when the relationship between Helena and Hermia developed, the friends (like their male antecedents) were inseparable, and marked by the extent of their likeness to one another, cf:

So we grew together,
Like to a double cherry, seeming parted,
But yet an union in partition,
Two lovely berries moulded on one stem;
So, with two seeming bodies, but one heart;
Two of the first, like coats in heraldry,
Due but to one, and crowned with one crest.

(III.ii.208–14)

In the eyes of the dramatis personae, the two girls, at the start of the play, still appear to be very similar. Theseus addresses Egeus' daughter as 'fair Hermia' (I.i.117) while Hermia salutes Nidar's as 'fair Helena' (I.i.180). Helena herself reflects at I.i.227 that 'through Athens I am thought as fair as she' (i.e. Hermia), while Demetrius contributes to the sense of their interchangeability by transferring his affections from one to the other. Seeing Helena in the forest, Oberon labels her a 'sweet Athenian lady' (II.i.260), a description that Puck has no difficulty in applying to her friend (II.ii.73–6). As the action progresses, however, the two women not only become estranged emotionally, but grow physically further apart, moving from their initial fairness towards the monstrous or grotesque. As noted above, Hermia becomes an 'Ethiope' in the eyes of Lysander (III.ii.257), while Hermia is transformed for Hermia from her 'sweet playfellow' (I.i.220) into a 'canker-blossom' (III.ii.282). At the same time, an emphasis upon the discrepancy between the stature of the two maidens becomes increasingly marked and is pushed to abnormal extremes. Helena, driven to 'impatient answers' (III.ii.287) by Hermia's accusations against her, refers to her former friend as a 'puppet' (III.ii.288), an epithet Hermia instantly assumes to be a reflection upon her height:

> 'Puppet'! Why, so? Ay, that way goes the game!
> Now I perceive that she hath made compare
> Between our statures; she hath urg'd her height;
> And with her personage, her tall personage,
> Her height, forsooth, she hath prevail'd with him [Lysander].
> And are you grown so high in his esteem
> Because I am so dwarfish and so low?
> How low am I, thou painted maypole? Speak:
> How low am I?

> (III.ii.289–97)

Here the stress upon 'tall' and 'height' serves to accentuate Helena's stature, while the terms 'low' and 'dwarfish' augment the physical distinction between the two women. At the same time, 'dwarfish' and 'maypole' imply deformity, or a movement away from human form, and this metamorphic process is sustained as the estrangement grows between the lovers. Helena describes Hermia as 'little' and 'fierce' (III.ii.325), the latter a term conventionally assigned to a beast, while Lysander rounds on the lady he formerly thought of as 'beauteous' (I.i.104) with:

> Get you gone, you dwarf;
> You minimus, of hindering knot-grass made;
> You bead, you acorn.

> (III.ii.328–30)

Here, Hermia descends not only in size but in position in the cosmic order. Having begun the play as a beautiful woman facing the cloister and thus a life in the service of God, she becomes unnaturally shaped, the most diminutive of beings, a troublesome weed, and an inanimate object. The diminution in her size to a 'bead' or 'acorn' serves to align her with the fairies rather than the Athenian world of the start of the play, and the same is true of her equation with aspects of the natural world (cf. Peaseblossom, Mustardseed). At the same time, Helena grows still further away from her in both form and nature. Her height, and the length of her legs, are emphasized (III.ii.303–5 and 343), while her self-confessed cowardice (III.ii.302) is at the furthest remove from Hermia's 'shrewishness' (III.ii.301). The fact that the smaller woman is courageous and the taller fearful also suggests a species of inversion, while the length of Helena's legs again aligns her with the creatures inhabiting the fairy world (cf. II.ii.20).

The metamorphosis that takes place in the perception of the friends corresponds to other shifts of form and vision that take place in the course of the play. Bottom is literally transformed, in part at least, into animal shape becoming an object of terror to his former companions, while captivating the fairy queen. Puck is instructed by Oberon to 'overcast the night' (III.ii.355), to 'frame [his] tongue' (III.ii.360) like Lysander's, and to 'rail' (II.ii.362) like Demetrius, thus convincing the two men that they are pursuing one another. The 'vile thing' (II.ii.33) of which Titania becomes enamoured is mirrored in the 'vile thing' (III.ii.260) Lysander rejects, while the grotesque misalliance between the fairy queen and an asinine mortal is echoed in the assimilation of the human lovers to subhuman forms.

The development of the love and friendship story from a paradigmatic exemplification of the superiority of asexual to sexual love to a strand in an escalating spiral of disorder is bound up in the role of passion in the play. Where Titus and Gisippus study philosophy and exemplify an ideal of amity that brings them closer to the divine, Helena and Hermia put their faith in an emotion that has little to do with the operations of the rational mind. Helena betrays Hermia for a man she knows to be inconstant, pursuing him through the wood regardless of his threats of violence towards her, while she appeals to the irrationality of sexual passion as justification for her conduct:

> Love looks not with the eyes, but with the mind,
> And therefore is wing'd Cupid painted blind;
> Nor hath Love's mind of any judgement taste:
> Wings, and no eyes, figure unheedy haste.
> And therefore is Love said to be a child,
> Because in choice he is so oft beguil'd.

(I.i.234–9)

As Bottom's response to Titania's declaration of her love for him indicates ('Methinks, mistress, you should have little reason for that. And yet, to say the truth, reason and love keep little company together nowadays', III.i.137–9) the attitudes of Helena and Hermia are typical of those in force in the world of the play. Theseus (a self-conscious advocate of rationality, cf. V.i.2–22) claims to have won Hippolyta's love 'by doing [her] injuries' (I.i.17); Oberon, in a jealous rage, causes his own queen to become besotted with a lesser being (cf. II.ii.26–33); while Egeus would prefer his daughter to lose her life than marry the (eminently suitable) man she has chosen as a husband (cf. I.i.38–45). The darkness in which much of the action takes place is emblematic of a lack of vision in the intellectual as well as the physical sense, while the wood in which the central scenes of the play are set is symbolic of the characters' mental confusion (cf. Spenser's wood in *The Faerie Queene*).

The dominance of passion over reason constitutes a perversion or dislocation of the natural order, and is associated, here as elsewhere, with an inversion of traditional sexual roles. The world of the intellect in the Renaissance is a conventionally male arena, while the emotions are associated with the theoretically less rational sex.[6] In locating his drama in a universe dominated by the passions rather than the intellect, Shakespeare is thus setting the action in an environment in which male and female are at odds, or the latter in ascendancy over the former. It is this aspect of the drama that makes *A Midsummer Night's Dream* particularly interesting for feminist criticism, and a significant text in the current debate over the dramatist's socio-political stance.

From the opening lines of the drama the audience is alerted both to the feminine arena in which the play is to function, and the discordant relationship that exists between female and male. Theseus, looking forward to his marriage to his bride-by-conquest, Hippolyta, evokes a world dominated by the moon (conventionally female) which he sees as inimical to the satisfaction of his desires:

> Now, fair Hippolyta, our nuptial hour
> Draws on apace; four happy days bring in
> Another moon: But O, methinks, how slow
> This old moon wanes! She lingers my desires,

6. For a full discussion of (and material illustrating) the ways in which the cultural concept of 'woman' was constructed during the Renaissance, see N.H.Keeble (1994) *The Cultural Identity of Seventeenth-Century Woman*, Routledge.

> Like to a step-dame or a dowager
> Long withering out a young man's revenue.

(I.i.1–6)

The imagery here, while conveying the strength of Theseus' desires and his enforced submission to the temporal process, defines authority in the world of the play as female, rather than male. The old moon, explicitly female, is seen as frustrating the happiness of the Duke, and is compared to other authority figures in atypical ascendancy over masculine dependents. Stepmothers (traditionally oppressive figures) are linked with 'dowagers' (women who have outlived their husbands and hold the purse strings in their hands) and both are seen by the speaker as adverse to male growth and development. Significantly, Hippolyta does not accept Theseus' account of the temporal process, though she too sees the moon as presiding over human affairs. For her,

> Four days will quickly steep themselves in night;
> Four nights will quickly dream away the time;
> And then the moon, like to a silver bow
> New bent in heaven, shall behold the night
> Of our solemnities.

(I.i.7–11)

Where Theseus sees the moon as a 'step-dame', or a 'dowager', defining the female in relation to the male, Hippolyta compares it to a 'silver bow', evocative of the goddess Diana, patroness of hunting and chastity, and consequently associated with female self-sufficiency.[7] While establishing the moonlight world of the drama, the lunar imagery employed here thus contributes to an understanding of the mental cast of the two speakers and helps to define the nature of their relationship. Theseus and Hippolyta are not courtly lovers. He has recently defeated her in battle, and the terms in which he refers to female dominance are negative, suggestive of his stance towards the relationship between the sexes. Conversely, she is a newly subjugated Amazon queen and her regret for her change of status is indicated by her sense of the rapid approach of her marriage, and lyrical evocation of the goddess of chastity.

The tension between male and female implicit in the opening lines is heightened with the entrance of Hermia and Egeus. Once again the relationship between the sexes constitutes a departure from the norm,

---

7. For an alternative reading of this passage as evocative of a fruitful union, see Harold F Brooks (ed.) (1979) *A Midsummer Night's Dream*, Arden edition, Methuen, p. 6n.

with a daughter resisting the wishes of a father, and then of the Duke. Egeus maintains that in his paternal role he is entitled to obedience (I.i.37), and that he has the authority to choose his daughter's husband (cf. 'As she is mine, I may dispose of her', I.i.42). Theseus confirms that in Hermia's eyes her father 'should be as a god' (I.i.47), and that it is fitting that she bow to his wishes. Hermia, however, not only repudiates her father's judgement, and resists the determination of the Duke, but declines to submit herself to the authority of Demetrius. Faced with a choice between the convent and an unwelcome marriage, she is unhesitating in her preference for a single life, a position clearly counter to the expectations of Theseus, who again, in seeking to persuade her, associates the moon (seen once more as female) with sexual frustration:

> The. Therefore, fair Hermia, question your desires,
> Know of your youth, examine well your blood,
> Whether, if you yield not to your father's choice,
> You can endure the livery of a nun,
> For aye to be in shady cloister mew'd,
> To live a barren sister all your life,
> Chanting faint hymns to the cold fruitless moon.
> Thrice blessed they that master so their blood
> To undergo such maiden pilgrimage;
> But earthlier happy is the rose distill'd
> Than that which, withering on the virgin thorn,
> Grows, lives, and dies, in single blessedness.
> Her. So will I grow, so live, so die, my lord,
> Ere I will yield my virgin patent up
> Unto his lordship whose unwished yoke
> My soul consents not to give sovereignty.
>
> (I.i.67–82)

The relationship between Oberon and Titania catches up a number of the sexual tensions initiated in the opening scene. Titania (who is associated once again with moonlight), refuses to defer to the authority of the fairy king, placing her affection for a 'votress of [her] order' (II.i.123) before the satisfaction of his wishes. The antagonism between the rulers of the fairy kingdom has been productive of cosmic disorder (cf. the earthly warfare between Theseus and Hippolyta), while Titania suggests that in bestowing his affections elsewhere Oberon has disrupted their sexual/hierarchical roles:

> Obe. Ill met by moonlight, proud Titania.
> Tita. What, jealous Oberon? Fairies, skip hence;

> I have forsworn his bed and company.
> Obe. Tarry, rash wanton; am not I thy lord?
> Tita. Then I must be thy lady; but I know
> When thou hast stolen away from fairy land,
> And in the shape of Corin, sat all day
> Playing on pipes of corn, and versing love
> To amorous Phillida. Why art thou here,
> Come from the farthest step of India,
> But that, forsooth, the bouncing Amazon,
> Your buskin'd mistress and your warrior love,
> To Theseus must be wedded?
>
> (II.i.60–72)

The play-within-the play performed by the mechanicals also contributes to the projection of a world in which conventional assumptions in relation to gender no longer hold good. Not only are the women's roles in the playlet overtly performed by men, thus endowing the characters with a quasi-masculine status,[8] but the heroine, like Hermia, meets her lover against her father's wishes, playing out her part by the light of the moon.

The shift of focus that Shakespeare effects in the love and friendship story is thus consonant with other strands of a drama in which traditional roles are resisted and the female usurps the authority of the male. At the same time, in transforming his faithful friends from men into women Shakespeare prioritizes female experience, and this process is evident in other areas of the play. Whereas in Elyot's tale the reader's attention is focused upon the decisions reached by Titus and Gisippus, and the conflicts that they undergo in the amatory arena, in Shakespeare's version of the story it is the situations of Helena and Hermia that are foregrounded, while Lysander and Demetrius, like the passive maidens of the archetype, are the victims of a process beyond their control. In the opening scene of the play, for example, though Lysander protests his love for Hermia, and reveals the fickleness of Demetrius, it is Hermia who is faced with the choice between an unwelcome marriage and the convent, and she who elects to trust to the probity of her lover. Similarly, though Demetrius expresses his love for Hermia and detestation of Helena, it is Helena who decides to place love before friendship, and thus secure Demetrius' company in the wood. Moreover, Helena makes her choice

---

8. All female roles in Shakespearian drama were, of course, originally performed by men. In the case of *Pyramus and Thisbe*, however, the masculinity of the actors is emphasized (cf. 'Let not me play a woman: I have a beard coming', I.ii.43–4), undermining the dramatic illusion.

in the only soliloquy that occurs in the course of the first scene, and is thus distinguished from the remainder of the characters who are observed solely in conversation. Once in the wood, the same process is repeated. Helena, deserted by Demetrius, laments her position by the sleeping Lysander, while the scene concludes with Hermia, deserted in turn by her lover, waking from a premonitory dream. Once again, Demetrius and Lysander respond to events rather than making decisions and neither is ever alone on the stage. The female characters of other strands of the drama are also given considerable prominence by the structuring of scenes. Oberon and Titania make their first entrance simultaneously, but it is she who dominates the dialogue with her lengthy account of the disorder consequent upon their division (II.i.81–117), and her explanation for her refusal to yield up the Indian boy (II.i.121–37). Similarly, II.ii opens with her entrance with her train, while III.i.124ff. is firmly located within the orbit of her fairy world. The interlude performed by the mechanicals, though dominated by Bottom, concludes not with Pyramus' death, but Thisbe's, the fate of the heroine occupying approximately a sixth of the entire play-within-the-play.

The foregrounding of Helena and Hermia among the young lovers, and the prominence afforded to female characters in other areas of the drama serves to align the audience in large measure with the predicaments of the play's women. With the exception of Oberon, the motives of the male characters remain largely unexplored, whereas the experiences of the women are more deeply rooted, explicable in terms of a pre-history reaching backwards beyond the opening of the play. Egeus' reasons for preferring the fickle Demetrius to the equally eligible Lysander, for example, are left unexplained, while Demetrius' infidelity, though it may be seen as part of the confusion instigated by the dissention between Titania and Oberon, is never explicitly accounted for. Even Oberon's motive for his conduct towards Titania appears disproportionate to the offence, in that his reasons for desiring the Indian boy as his henchman have to be inferred rather than being fully stated. Conversely, Helena's situation, rejected by Demetrius and then seemingly scorned by her friends, is much more fully realized (cf. I.i.226–51 and III.ii.192ff.), while Titania's motives for withholding the changeling boy are poignantly elaborated, and invite a sympathetic response:

> His mother was a votress of my order;
> And in the spiced Indian air, by night,
> Full often hath she gossip'd by my side;

And sat with me on Neptune's yellow sands,
Marking th'embarked traders on the flood:
When we have laugh'd to see the sails conceive
And grow big-bellied with the wanton wind;
Which she, with pretty and with swimming gait
Following (her womb then rich with my young squire),
Would imitate, and sail upon the land
To fetch me trifles, and return again
As from a voyage rich with merchandise.
But she, being mortal, of that boy did die;
And for her sake do I rear up her boy;
And for her sake I will not part with him.

(II.i.123–37)

Where Oberon's stance appears arbitrary and vindictive, the attitudes expressed here are comprehensible and rooted in affection. The situation she depicts is one of intimacy (cf. 'gossip'd), caring (cf. 'for her sake'), and creativity (cf. 'conceive', 'big-bellied', 'womb', 'rear up'), while the world she evokes is full of perfume and colour (cf. 'spiced Indian air', 'yellow sands') in striking contrast to that conjured up by Oberon's spell in the following scene (cf. II.ii.26–33).

The attitude of the audience towards the play world as a whole is reflected in Oberon's stance towards the human lovers. Functioning as an internal audience to the drama played out among the mortals, he aligns himself with Helena rather than Demetrius, seeing the former as 'a sweet Athenian lady' and the latter as 'a disdainful youth' (II.i.260–1). Similarly Puck, finding Hermia and Lysander sleeping, and mistaking them for Helena and Demetrius, views one as a 'pretty soul' and the other as a 'churl' (II.ii.75 and 77), commenting, as he later watches the exhausted lovers fall asleep, that 'Cupid is a knavish lad / Thus to make poor females mad' (III.ii.440–1).

The focus on female experience in the play affords a perspective upon the interaction between the sexes that reflects adversely on male-dominated institutions, and it is this fact that has attracted the notice of feminist criticism.[9] Whereas, in the story of Titus and Gisippus, the woman renounced by one friend in favour of the other is merely a focus for the conflict between love and friendship and thus a two-dimensional figure with no point of view, Shakespeare's women are given a voice and a freedom of action that challenges the validity of male authority in

9. See, for example, Jeanne Addison Roberts (1991) *The Shakespearean Wild: Geography, Genus, Gender*, University of Nebraska Press, pp.178ff.

the play world. Theseus, for example, has forced rather than persuaded Hippolyta to be his bride, and there is nothing in her conduct to suggest that she is in any way his natural inferior. Titania describes her as a 'warrior' (II.i.71) suggesting her capacity to function in a male arena, while her dissent from the attitudes of the society she has entered is evident at more than one point. Theseus' anxious 'what cheer my love?' (I.i.122) after the judgement he passes on Hermia, suggests that she is ill at ease with the choice that he has imposed upon the younger woman, while she shows greater understanding than her future husband in their later discussion of the lovers' story, adopting a position fundamentally at odds with his (cf. V.i.1–27).

It is the figures of Egeus and Oberon, however, and their relationship to Hermia and Titania that afford the most striking evidence in favour of the feminist sympathies of the play. Egeus, who would rather see his daughter die than dissent from his wishes, is an unappealing figure, whereas Hermia pleading to be allowed some say in deciding to whom she should 'yield her virgin patent up' (I.i.80) is more sympathetic, particularly in view of the deficiencies of her father's choice. The patriarchal system (embodied in Theseus), which Egeus successfully invokes, is called into question by the cogency of the young lovers' position and by the inherent destructiveness of Egeus' stance, and the same can be argued of Oberon's assertion of his authority over Titania. As noted above, her reasons for resisting his wishes are sympathetically treated, while his enforcement of what appears an arbitrary whim is both demeaning and malicious. Male authority, in short, resides here not in an inherent superiority of judgement, but the power to coerce, and the play is notable for the frequency of its references to violence, including more than one allusion to rape (cf. II.i.74–8 and 214–19).

While the prioritization of female experience and the oppressive actions of patriarchal figures permit the play to be interpreted as exhibiting a proto-feminist stance, the conclusion lends support to that school of criticism that sees the strategies of Renaissance drama in terms of subversion and containment. For all the prominence of the female characters and the physical and intellectual energy that they exhibit, by the closing scenes of the drama they are effectively disempowered. The marriage between Theseus and Hippolyta, impending at the outset, is accomplished by the end of the play, transforming the Amazon Queen (i.e. one with a distinctive area of operation) into the consort of another ruler. Hermia and Helena are re-assimilated into the social system that the former had challenged through their marriages to Lysander and

Demetrius, while Titania yields up the Indian boy to Oberon, and accepts him once again as her 'lord' (cf. IV.i.98). Moreover, Titania's long speech on the disorder consequent upon her quarrel with Oberon permits the events of the drama to be viewed as the anarchic consequences of disruption in the supernatural sphere. The perverse courtship of Theseus, Demetrius' repudiation of Helena, Egeus' destructive anger towards Hermia and his daughter's rejection of his authority, Helena's dogged pursuit of Demetrius and his threats of violence towards her, are all capable of interpretation as evidence of the topsy-turvy world the fairies have brought into being, a world governed by passion rather than reason, in which the daylight clarity of the rational mind has given way to darkness and the confusion of dream. With the renewal of concord in the fairy kingdom, cosmic order is restored and that process is reflected in the re-establishment of patriarchal authority. Theseus presides at the close of the drama over a harmonious, hierarchical court, its joyousness implying that the position achieved by the final scene is a natural one and that the period of female emancipation was, in consequence, an aberration.

The polarized accounts of *A Midsummer Night's Dream* offered by the interpretations outlined above are indicative of the resistance of Shakespearian drama to single socio-political readings, and the multivalency of the dramatist's treatment of the love and friendship story is evident to the final moments of the play. Whereas the drama culminates in marriage, and celebrates the re-establishment of a hierarchical society, it is evident to the audience, if not the dramatis personae, that the order that is finally instituted is not that initially ordained by Theseus, nor is it rooted in a traditionally masculine value system. For all his original judgement upon Hermia, Theseus consents to her marriage to Lysander, overriding both the laws of Athens and the wishes of Egeus. Helena betrays friendship for love and succeeds in winning Demetrius, contrary to the convention from which her position derives, while it is beings of the night, capable of transgressing the laws of logic, who are ultimately responsible for earthly harmony. At the close of the play, it is not the well-regulated mind, trained in philosophy, that enables the social order to be re-established, but a vindictive, self-harming stratagem on the part of a jealous spirit; the play concludes not in daylight but with the roar of the hungry lion (V.i.357), the cry of the screech-owl (V.i.362), and the promise of 'nightly revels' (V.i.356); while it is notable that watching the tragedy of Pyramus and Thisbe, the Amazonian bride, Hippolyta, is quick to applaud the moon.

Chapter 4

Measure for Measure and the Tale of the Heroic Sacrifice

And after these things God did prove Abraham, and said
unto him, Abraham: who answered, here am I.

And he said, Take thine only son Isaac, whom thou lovest and
get thee unto the land of Moriah; and offer him there for
a burnt offering upon one of the mountains which I will show thee.

Then Abraham rose up early in the morning, and saddled his ass, and
took two of his servants with him, and Isaac his son, and clove
wood for the burnt offering, and rose up, and went to the place
which God had told him.

Then the third day Abraham lift up his eyes, and saw the place
afar off.

And said unto his servants, Abide you here with the ass; for
I and the child will go yonder and worship, and come again unto you.

Then Abraham took the wood of the burnt offering, and laid it upon
Isaac his son; and he took the fire in his hand, and the knife; and
they went both together.

Then spake Isaac unto Abraham his father, and said, My father: and
he answered, Here am I, my son. And he said, Behold the fire and
the wood, but where is the lamb for the burnt offering?

Then Abraham answered, My son, God will provide him a lamb for a
burnt offering: so they went both together.

And when they came to the place which God had showed him, Abraham
builded an altar there, and couched the wood, and bound Isaac
his son, and laid him on the altar upon the wood.

And Abraham, stretching forth his hand, took the knife to kill
his son.

But the angel of the Lord called unto him from heaven, saying
Abraham, Abraham: and he answered, Here am I.

Then he said, Lay not thine hand upon the child, neither do thou any

thing unto him: for now I know that thou fearest God, seeing for my
sake thou hast not spared thine only son.

And Abraham, lifting up his eyes, looked, and behold there was a
ram behind [him] caught by the horns in a bush. Then Abraham went
and took the ram, and offered him up for a burnt offering in the
stead of his son.

The tale of Abraham and Isaac (*Genesis*, 22:1–13) draws together a number of motifs underlying a tissue of traditional stories, deeply rooted in
many instances in religious observance. An authority figure, often a
deity, demands the sacrifice of an object of supreme value, but provides
or accepts a substitute once the obedience of the subject has been established. The pattern of the tale has obvious analogies with the Christian
doctrine of the atonement, and the Abraham/Isaac story itself was frequently read, from early in the history of the Christian church, as a
prefiguration of the sacrifice of Christ for the sins of the world, with
God demanding the death of mankind as a consequence of the fall, but
accepting his son[1] in humanity's place. In assimilating the story into the
western European theological tradition, however, Christian exegesists
effected a significant shift in its emphasis. Whereas the Judaic version of
the story focuses upon the heroic behaviour of the father in his willingness to offer up his son, the Christian reading stresses, not the sacrifice of
the father figure (in this instance God), but the heroism of the son in
yielding his life on mankind's behalf. Where the Judaic story is one of
obedience, the Christian tale is one of love, its moral expounded by
Christ himself in the Gospel according to St John:

As the Father hath loved me, so have I loved you; continue in
my love.

If ye shall keep my commandments, ye shall abide in my love; as
I have kept my Father's commandments, and abide in his love.

These things have I spoken unto you, that my joy might remain
in you, and that your joy might be full.

This is my commandment, That ye love one another, as I have
loved you.

Greater love than this hath no man, when any man bestoweth his life
for his friends.

Ye are my friends, if ye do whatsoever I command you.

(*St John*, 15:9–14)

---

1. The phrase 'the lamb of God', frequently used in Christian discourse with reference to
   Christ, supports (on one level) the association with the Abraham and Isaac story
   through the concept of a sacrificial offering.

While Christ's words here register his readiness to lay down his life
on behalf of his disciples, they also impose an obligation upon those
who follow his teachings to model their conduct upon his own. To sacrifice one's life on behalf of a friend is to re-enact the conduct of the
Saviour, and thus becomes a pattern in Christian literature of exemplary
behaviour. Numerous stories current in both the Middle Ages and the
Renaissance (many adapted from the classical stock) offer examples of
this variety of heroic conduct. In Boccaccio's story of Titus and
Gisippus (*Decameron*, Day 10, Story 8), for example, Titus confesses to a
murder he has not committed when his friend Gisippus is wrongly
accused of the crime, the self-sacrificing love between the two men
causing the magistrate to seek a means of pardoning both, and prompting the true murderer to confess to his guilt. The tale is re-told by Sir
Thomas Elyot in *The Boke Named the Governour* (see above, Chapter 3,
passim) as an example of the kind of conduct expected of the ideal
Renaissance man, and dramatized versions of similar stories appear at an
early date on the Renaissance stage. Richard Edwards' *Damon and
Pithias* (1565), for example, a play written for performance by boys and
based upon a classical story, is again concerned with a pair of friends,
one of whom (like Gisippus) is arrested for a crime of which he is innocent, but who is allowed to return to his home in order to settle his
affairs, on condition that the other stands surety for his return. Delayed
by unforeseen circumstances, the accused man arrives as his friend is
about to be put to death, and the two then contend over which of them
should die. A similar pattern underlies Shakespeare's *The Merchant of
Venice* (1596–8) in which the Christian resonances of the story are
implicit in the conflict that the drama sets up between the members of a
Renaissance community and a Jewish usurer, Shylock. A Christian merchant, Antonio, guarantees a loan for his friend, Bassanio, with a pound
of his own flesh, and the terms in which the two men express their
readiness to sacrifice themselves for one another, when the bond is for-
feit, are rich in theological implications, cf:

> Por[tia]. You merchant, have you anything to say?
> Ant[onio]. But little; I am arm'd and well prepar'd, –
> Give me your hand Bassanio, fare you well,
> Grieve not that I am fall'n to this for you:
> For herein Fortune shows herself more kind
> Than is her custom: it is still her use
> To let the wretched man outlive his wealth,
> To view with hollow eye and wrinkled brow

An age of poverty: from which ling'ring penance
Of such misery doth she cut me off.
Commend me to your honourable wife,
Tell her the process of Antonio's end,
Say how I lov'd you, speak me fair in death:
And when the tale is told, bid her be judge
Whether Bassanio had not once a love:
Repent but you that you shall lose your friend
And he repents not that he pays your debt.
For if the Jew do cut but deep enough,
I'll pay it instantly with all my heart.
Bass[anio]. Antonio, I am married to a wife
Which is as dear to me as life itself,
But life itself, my wife, and all the world,
Are not with me esteem'd above thy life.
I would lose all, ay sacrifice them all
Here to this devil, to deliver you.

(The Merchant of Venice, IV.i.259–83)

Though frequently assimilated to the love and friendship tradition as the above examples suggest, tales involving a supreme sacrifice in Renaissance literature are not exclusively concerned with male experience. For women, however, the act of laying down on behalf of a loved one is frequently literal, rather than figurative, and takes place in a private rather than a public context. Many stories in Renaissance collections turn on the predicament of a virtuous woman called upon to sacrifice her chastity to preserve the life of a male relative, and the exploitation, not only of her person, but her trust. In the tale of Epitia and Juriste, for example, related in Decade 8, Novella 5 of Geraldo Cinthio's *Hecatommithi* (1565), Epitia intercedes with the Governor Juriste on behalf of her brother who has committed a rape, and finds herself faced with a choice between her virginity and her brother's safety. Having yielded to the Governor's lust, she is then presented with her brother's head, and is forced to seek redress from a higher authority. The story was retold by George Whetsone in his *Heptameron of Civill Discourses* (1582), and a similar tale occurs in Part II of Thomas Lupton's *Too Good to be True* (1581), in which the corrupt judge again reneges on the agreement made with the lady, in this instance to spare the life of her husband. For all its popularity in the sixteenth century, however, the story is not Renaissance in origin, but is found in Christian literature as early as the *De Sermone Domini in Monte Secundum Matthaeum* of St Augustine of Hippo (345–430) where it is used as an illustration of the difficulty of passing absolute judgements in cases of marital infidelity. Augustine relates the example of a woman whose husband's life is under threat because of his inability to pay a debt, and who lies with a rich man, at her husband's request, in exchange for the money to obtain his freedom. As in many later versions of the story, the blackmailer fails to keep his word, and the lady is obliged for love of her husband to publish her own shame in a final effort to obtain redress.

Though the issues explored through the story vary from writer to writer (Augustine, for example, is interested in the complex nature of moral issues, whereas Cinthio is concerned with the relationship between justice and mercy) in each instance the moral predicament faced by a noble woman lies at the heart of the story, and the heroic sacrifice that she makes on behalf of another functions as an index of her virtue. The title page of George Whetstone's *Promos and Cassandra*, for example, a two-part play published in 1578, announces that the drama is concerned with 'the virtuous behaviours of a chaste lady',[2] and the 'Argument' stresses the magnanimity of the heroine both in submitting to the embraces of Promos in order to win her brother's freedom, and in pleading for the life of her betrayer once he has been obliged to become her husband. Whetstone's drama is significant, moreover, not only in the stress that it lays upon the virtue of the heroine, but in the fact that it combines, like the Abraham and Isaac story, the concept of the heroic sacrifice with the provision of a substitute offering. Not only does Cassandra consent, like Abraham, to surrender an object of supreme value, but a higher power intercedes to avert a threatened death by furnishing an acceptable alternative. Though Promos orders the execution of her brother once Cassandra has submitted to his will, the jailor 'by the providence of God' declines to carry out his wishes, providing 'a felon's head newly executed'[3] in Andrugio's place.

Whether of life, as in the case of men, or sexual honour, as in the case of women, the sacrifices made in these stories testify to the love or dutifulness of the central figures, and are performed willingly, if not with gladness of heart. Just as Abraham unquestioningly prepares his son for the sacrifice at God's injunction, and Christ lays down his life unreservedly for man, so the faithful comrades of the love and friendship tradition are swift to offer their lives for one another, while the female

---

2. Quoted from Geoffrey Bullough (1957–75) *Narrative and Dramatic Sources of Shakespeare*, vol. ii, Routledge and Kegan Paul, p. 442. All subsequent quotations from the play are based on this edition, but spelling and punctuation have been modernized.
3. Ibid., p. 445.

relatives faced with the loss of their loved ones, unhesitatingly yield up their bodies for a husband or brother's salvation. The acceptance by all parties of the probity of the sacrifice testifies to a clearly defined value system understood (and endorsed) by the audience to whom these works are addressed. The tales posit a patriarchal universe in which the individual's prime duty is to God, to others, and in the case of women, to the male members of the family group, and imply a clear hierarchy of rights and duties. Just as the proper relationship between God and mankind is exhibited through a willing obedience to the divine behest, and the ideal conduct of the Christian gentleman is displayed through the re-enactment of the sacrifice of Christ, so the appropriate relationship between man and woman is reflected in female submission to male authority, with the willing surrender of the person a lower link in the chain of sacrificial acts. Whether yielding up a son, a life, or a maidenhead, the characters of these stories conform, through their actions, to the workings of an ideal world, and it is the assumptions underlying their conduct that are challenged in Shakespeare's alternative version of the tale.

Measure for Measure (1604) draws on a variety of sources in the construction of a complex web of substitution motifs.[4] The action is set in motion by the Duke's nomination of Angelo as his deputy during his apparent absence from the city, and it is notable that this first act of substitution is met with a measure of resistance. Rather than expressing his gratitude for the honour accorded him, Angelo voices doubts as to his fitness for the office, and a sense of unreadiness for the challenge it represents:

> Now, good my lord,
> Let there be some more test made of my metal,
> Before so noble and so great a figure
> Be stamp'd upon it.
>
> (I.i.47–50)

The reluctance that he exhibits to assume the required part is characteristic of the action that follows. In enforcing a law against fornication he causes a young man, Claudio, to be arrested for sleeping with his betrothed wife, and it is at this point that Shakespeare turns to one of

---

4. For a detailed account of the materials drawn on in the construction of the play see Bullough, *Narrative and Dramatic Sources of Shakespeare*, vol. ii, pp. 399ff. and J.W. Lever (ed.) (1965) *Measure for Measure*, The Arden Shakespeare, Methuen, pp. xxxv–lv.

the heroic sacrifice motifs outlined above. Isabella, Claudio's sister, intercedes on her brother's behalf, and is solicited by Angelo to exchange her virginity for his freedom. Like the wives and sisters of the sources from which the action derives Isabella initially condemns the proposal, but the terms in which she does so mark a departure from the traditional story in that they mount a counter-argument to the value system assumed in the inherited tale:

> Ang[elo]. Admit no other way to save his life –
> As I subscribe not that, nor any other,
> But in the loss of question – that you, his sister,
> Finding yourself desir'd of such a person
> Whose credit with the judge, or own great place,
> Could fetch your brother from the manacles
> Of the all-binding law: and that there were
> No earthly mean to save him, but that either
> You must lay down the treasures of your body
> To this suppos'd, or else to let him suffer:
> What would you do?
> Isab[ella]. As much for my poor brother as myself;
> That is, were I under the terms of death,
> Th'impression of keen whips I'd wear as rubies,
> And strip myself to death as to a bed
> That longing have been sick for, ere I'd yield
> My body up to shame.
> Ang.   Then must your brother die.
> Isab. And 'twere the cheaper way.
> Better it were a brother died at once,
> Than that a sister, by redeeming him,
> Should die for ever.
> Ang. Were you not then as cruel as the sentence
> That you have slander'd so?
> Isab. Ignominy in ransom and free pardon
> Are of two houses: lawful mercy
> Is nothing kin to foul redemption.

(II.iv.88–113)

The position adopted here challenges the assumption that the sacrifice of female honour for male safety constitutes an admirable course of conduct. In weighing up the alternative evils confronting her Isabella juxtaposes earthly (Claudio's) against spiritual (her own) death, rejecting the price demanded of her as inadmissible, and in doing so shifting the emphasis of the story from the heroic deed performed by the heroine to the implications of that action for both parties in the transaction. Where the husbands and brothers of the source material are largely the embodiments of a predicament salvable only by the self-sacrificing conduct of another, Claudio is drawn more deeply into the situation, potentially contaminated by the very action (cf. 'foul redemption') designed, in theory, to expunge his offence. Isabella's stance at the close of the scene, moreover, prepares for a yet more radical departure from the process enacted in the traditional tale. Rather than feeling trapped by her situation, she turns instantly to her brother, placing sexual (and implicitly family) honour before masculine safety, confident that Claudio will endorse her position:

> I'll to my brother.
> Though he hath fall'n by prompture of the blood,
> Yet hath he in him such a mind of honour,
> That had he twenty heads to tender down
> On twenty bloody blocks, he'd yield them up
> Before his sister should her body stoop
> To such abhorr'd pollution.
> Then, Isabel live chaste, and brother, die:
> More than our brother is our chastity.
> I'll tell him yet of Angelo's request,
> And fit his mind to death, for his soul's rest.
>
> (II.iv.176–86)

The assurance that Isabella exhibits here that Claudio will share her priorities turns the potential for sacrifice between the siblings into a two-way exchange, further problematizing the nature of right action, and contributing to the division of interest between brother and sister. Where Angelo invites Isabella to offer herself on Claudio's behalf, Isabella expects her brother to give his life rather than sacrifice her honour, evoking chivalric concepts of exemplary behaviour, and thus calling conflicting notions of right conduct into play.

Just as Isabella, however, repudiates the sacrifice required of her by Angelo, so Claudio fails to fulfil the part assigned to him by his sister. Acquainted by Isabella in III.i. with the conditions propounded for his release, he instinctively rejects the terms of his ransom only to waver in his resolution when he reflects upon the terrors of death:

> Isab.   This night's the time
> That I should do what I abhor to name;
> Or else thou diest tomorrow.
> Cla.   Thou shalt not do't.

Isab. O, were it but my life,
   I'd throw it down for your deliverance
   As frankly as a pin.
Cla.   Thanks, dear Isabel.
Isab. Be ready, Claudio, for your death tomorrow.
Cla. Yes. – Has he affections in him,
   That thus can make him bite the law by th'nose
   When he would force it? – Sure, it is no sin;
   Or of the deadly seven it is the least.
Isab. Which is the least?
Cla. If it were damnable, he being so wise,
   Why would he for the momentary trick
   Be perdurably fin'd? – O Isabel!
Isab. What says my brother?
Cla.   Death is a fearful thing.
Isab. And shamed life a hateful.
Cla. Ay, but to die, and go we know not where;
   To lie in cold obstruction, and to rot;
   This sensible warm motion to become
   A kneaded clod; and the delighted spirit
   To bath in fiery floods, or to reside
   In thrilling region of thick-ribbed ice;
   To be imprison'd in the viewless winds
   And blown with restless violence round about
   The pendant world: or to be worse than worst
   Of those that lawless and incertain thought
   Imagine howling, – 'tis too horrible.
   The weariest and most loathed worldly life
   That age, ache, penury and imprisonment
   Can lay on nature, is a paradise
   To what we fear of death.
Isab.   Alas, alas!
Cla. Sweet sister, let me live.

                           (III.i.100–32)

The fullness of Claudio's response here serves to flesh out his role in the story, while contributing to the moral uncertainty of the situation that the dramatist sets up. On the one hand, his fear of death is sympathetic, and his plea to Isabella a deeply moving one, while on the other his lack of resolution and willingness to sacrifice his sister convict him of a failure to conform to traditional concepts of masculine virtue and thus to merit the conventional act of self-surrender. Whereas the condemned brother of *Promos and Cassandra* argues the moral propriety of the action and stresses the danger that his loss would represent to the family group,[5] Claudio's appeal is based not on probity but on fear, undermining his stature and creating a tension between a hypothetical world in which male superiority commands the dutiful submission of the female sex, and the real world in which men may be morally reprehensible, and thus unworthy of unqualified respect. At the same time, Isabella puts forward a set of priorities that run counter to those of the inherited story, and invert gender expectations. Whereas Claudio is caught up in the terror of dying, his sister affirms her willingness to yield up her life in order to save him, overturning conventional assumptions regarding the relative courageousness of the sexes while implying that the traditionally superior male sacrifice of life is, in fact, a lesser one than the female surrender of the person with its connotations of sin.

The progressive inversion of audience expectation effected in the course of the two scenes reaches a climax in Isabella's response to her brother's plea to perform the requisite self-abnegating action on his behalf. Rather than yielding, like her romance progenitors, to male persuasion, she rounds vehemently upon him, repudiating both Claudio himself and the proposed exchange in the most vigorous terms:

> O, you beast!
> O faithless coward! O dishonest wretch!
> Wilt thou be made a man out of my vice?
> Is't not a kind of incest, to take life
> From thine own sister's shame? What should I think?
> Heaven shield my mother play'd my father fair:
> For such a warped slip of wilderness
> Ne'er issued from his blood. Take my defiance,
> Die, perish! Might but my bending down

---

5. Cf. Cassandra, if thou thyself submit,
   To save my life, to Promos fleshly will,
   Justice will say thou dost no crime commit:
   For in forced faults is no intent of ill.

   ...

   Sweet sister, more slander would infame
   Your spotless life, to reave your brother's breath
   When you have power for to enlarge the same,
   Once in your hands doth lie my life and death.
   Weigh that I am the self same flesh you are,
   Think, I once gone, our house will go to wrack:
   Know forced faults, for slander need not care:
   Look you for blame if I quail through your lack.

                                                    (Part I, III.iv.33–52)

Reprieve thee from thy fate, it should proceed.
I'll pray a thousand prayers for thy death;
No word to save thee.

                                                        (III.i.135–46)

Not only is Isabella's position here at the furthest possible remove from that of the wives and sisters of the inherited story, making it very difficult for the audience to imagine how the situation can be resolved, it also challenges the basic premise underlying the course of conduct on which her predecessors are persuaded to engage. Rather than stressing the heroic nature of surrendering the self on behalf of another, the lines focus upon the degeneracy of a mind willing to buy life on such terms (cf. 'coward', 'dishonest', 'warped'), and thus interrogate the ideological assumptions underpinning the conventional tale. At the same time, however, the sympathetic nature of Claudio's appeal, and the vehemency of his sister's rejection, frustrate an unqualified alignment with the stance that Isabella adopts. Rather than upholding an alternative value system, the play complicates the process of judgement, dividing the sympathies of the audience between brother and sister and thus translating the drama from a paradigmatic universe with an agreed value system into a world of conflicting impulses in which the propriety of an action is not readily assessed.

The solution propounded by the Duke to resolve the impasse between the siblings draws on a second strand of the complex of tales outlined at the start of this chapter, and once again subverts the inherited motif. Just as God in the tale of Abraham and Isaac supplies a substitute for the designated sacrifice in the shape of the ram caught in the bush by its horns, and the providentially inspired jailor of *Promos and Cassandra* averts the death of the heroine's brother (after the sexual ransom has been paid) by furnishing the corrupt judge with another man's head, so the Duke engineers a replacement for Isabella in Angelo's bed in order to salvage both Claudio's life and the heroine's honour. Unlike the traditional story, however, in which the provision of the substitute sacrifice constitutes a reward for right conduct exhibited through the willing surrender of an object of value, in *Measure for Measure* the Duke's device is not a recompense for heroic virtue but a desperate recourse, in that the theoretically commendable course of action is not pursued. Since Isabella repudiates the invitation to yield up her body on Claudio's behalf, the Duke is obliged to find an alternative offering in order to avert a tragic outcome, rather than supplying one as an act of grace. The course proposed to Isabella's substitute is not propounded, moreover, in terms of an altruistic act (cf. the competition between Damon and Pithias over which should die on the other's behalf), but as personal fulfilment, and the righting of a wrong. Previously betrothed to Angelo, Mariana (Isabella's substitute) becomes his wife on being admitted to his bed,[6] wiping out the shame of her rejection rather than being contaminated by an act of violation. An exemplary process (heroic action leading to public approval or divine reward) is thus transformed into a self-interested transaction in a world in which expediency, rather than conformity to a shared ideology, governs human conduct.

While Isabella's refusal to conform to the pattern of behaviour predicated by the inherited plot implicitly challenges the assumptions of a patriarchal society, the outcome of the Duke's stratagem leads to a more far-reaching interrogation of the socio-ideological structure upon which the meaning of the conventional tale depends. Though convinced that Isabella has fulfilled the terms imposed for her brother's release, Angelo fails, like his romance counterparts, to keep his side of the bargain, fearful of the revenge that Claudio might exact on his sister's behalf (cf. IV.iv.26–30). The Duke is consequently obliged to intervene, once again, to avert disaster, seeking to furnish (like the jailor in *Promos and Cassandra*) a surrogate head for that of the threatened man. It is at this point in the action that Shakespeare achieves his most complex alternative version of the sources on which he draws, combining in a single figure both the heroic and substitute sacrifice motifs. Whereas the jailor in *Promos and Cassandra* quickly secures an acceptable replacement by means of a previous decapitation, the Duke turns to a living prisoner, Barnardine, in order to supply the substitute offering, effectively calling on him to die, like the faithful friends of *The Boke Named the Governour* or *Damon and Pithias*, on another's behalf. Unlike the ideal gentlemen of sixteenth-century literature (or their divine antecedent), however, Barnardine declines (like Isabella) to perform the expected part, the brief scene in which he figures constituting one of the most unsettling elements of a drama that insistently plays against audience expectation.

Though he appears only twice in the course of the action (IV.iii.36ff. and V.i.476ff.), Barnardine's character and situation are established in some detail at the point at which the need for a dead man's head is first introduced. Anticipating an order for Claudio's release, the Duke is

---

6. Betrothal became absolute marriage in the eyes of both church and state during the Elizabethan-Jacobean period when the relationship between the couple was consummated.

present when the Provost receives the unexpected instruction to proceed with the execution, and thus hears, via Angelo himself, of the existence of a second condemned man:

> Prov[ost]. [Reads] *Whatsoever you may hear to the*
> *contrary, let Claudio be executed by four of the clock, and in the*
> *afternoon, Barnardine. For my better satisfaction, let me have*
> *Claudio's head sent me by five. Let this be duly performed,*
> *with a thought that more depends on it than we must yet deliver.*
>
> (IV.ii.118–23)

For the members of the theatre audience these instructions carry the hope of a solution to the quandary in which the dramatis personae are placed. The coincidental timing of the executions suggests the providential provision of a human scapegoat, and the Duke's swift response to the letter confirms the spectators' expectations that Barnardine's head will be substituted for that of the other imprisoned man:

> Duke. What is that Barnardine, who is to be executed in
> th'afternoon?
> Prov. A Bohemian born, but here nursed up and bred;
> one that is a prisoner nine years old.
> Duke. How came it that the absent Duke had not either
> delivered him to his liberty, or executed him? I
> have heard it was ever his manner to do so.
> Prov. His friends still wrought reprieves for him; and
> indeed, his fact till now in the government of Lord
> Angelo came not to an undoubtful proof.
> Duke. Is it now apparent?
> Prov. Most manifest, and not denied by himself.
> Duke. Hath he borne himself penitently in prison?
> How seems he to be touched?
> Prov. A man that apprehends death no more dreadfully
> but as a drunken sleep; careless, reckless, and fear-
> less of what's past, present, or to come: insensible of
> mortality, and desperately mortal.
> Duke. He wants advice.
> Prov. He will hear none. He hath evermore had the liberty
> of the prison: give him leave to escape hence, he would not.
> Drunk many times a day, if not many days entirely drunk.
> We have very oft awaked him, as if to carry him to execution,
> and showed him a seeming warrant for it: it hath not moved him
> at all.
>
> ...

Duke. Let this Barnardine be this morning executed, and his
head borne to Angelo.

Prov. Angelo hath seen them both, and will discover the
favour.

Duke. O, death's a great disguiser; and you may add to it.
Shave the head, and tie the beard, and say it was the
desire of the penitent to be so bared before his death:
you know the course is common.

(IV.ii.126–77)

The very fullness of this exchange serves to confirm audience expectation that Barnardine will afford the means of Claudio's salvation. The
Provost's account sets up a systematic correspondence between the two
figures that permits the spectator to view them as antithetical versions of
one another, and thus justifies their transposition. The execution of
both men has been delayed by the intercession of friends, but in all
other respects they stand at opposite ends of the social and moral spectrum. Barnardine is a foreigner, a prisoner of long standing, guilty of a
crime to which he admits, whereas Claudio is a newly arrested citizen,
whose offence against the state is of a purely technical kind. The attitudes of the two men to their situations, moreover, are diametrically
opposed. Claudio is fearful of the grave and acutely aware of the value
of life (cf. III.i.117–31, quoted above), whereas Barnardine 'apprehends
death no more dreadfully but as a drunken sleep' (IV.ii.140–1) and has
no interest in escaping his prison. More pertinently, a pointed contrast is
established between the two prisoners' moral condition. Claudio,
though he is guilty of anticipating the formal celebration of his nuptials,
and errs in his attempt to exploit his sister's affection, repents of his
errors and submits to spiritual correction (cf. III.i.5–43 and 165–71),
whereas Barnardine refuses to listen to counsel of any kind. At the same
time the description of the two men sets up a distance between them in
terms of the fullness of their humanity. Claudio is a young man, with a
betrothed wife who is expecting his child, and a sister to whom he is
clearly attached. His prison speeches betray an acute mind, and a vivid
imagination, while the terms in which he speaks of his offence (cf.
I.ii.112–22) reveal a highly developed moral nature. Barnardine, by
contrast, is an isolated figure, who has been in prison for nine years and
has no interest in the world beyond his cell. The fact that he is 'insensi-
ble of mortality' (IV.ii.142–3) implies a want of human perception,
while his continual drunkenness denotes the overthrow of reason. His
imperviousness to the mental tricks played upon him suggests an animal

condition, and this inference is heightened by his willingness to remain within the confines of the prison, and indifference to any means of escape. In short, the exchange between the Duke and the Provost establishes Barnardine as one who has sunk to the level of a beast, and who may therefore be fitly exchanged, like the ram in the thicket, for a member of the human community.

The close of the scene serves to heighten audience conviction that the substitution will be carried out, while contributing to the sense of its propriety. The Duke speaks decisively, and with an air of authority, intimating a new control over the progress of events:

> Put not yourself into amazement how these things should be;
> all difficulties are but easy when they are known. Call
> your executioner, and off with Barnardine's head. I will
> give him a present shrift, and advise him for a better place.
> Yet you [the Provost] are amazed; but this shall absolutely
> resolve you. Come away; it is almost clear dawn.

(IV.ii.203–9)

The words mark a reassertion of the Duke's temporal and spiritual power, while the reference to dawn in the closing line carries the suggestion that the metaphorical darkness of the action will also be dispelled. Any concern for the fate of the condemned prisoner is allayed by the assurance that he will be cleansed before death of his sins, and that he is about to exchange a demeaning captivity for 'a better place'.

The entrance of Abhorson, the executioner, in the following scene, and his brief conversation with Pompey, the jailor, sustains the belief that the sentence will be carried out, while contributing to the image of the condemned man projected in the previous scene. Barnardine is sleeping after a night's drinking, and the two men find it difficult to rouse him:

> Abhor. Sirrah, bring Barnardine hither.
> Pom. Master Barnardine! You must rise and be hanged, Master
>   Barnardine.
> Abhor. What hoa, Barnardine!
> Barnardine. [*within.*] A pox o' your throats! Who makes that
>   noise there? What are you?
> Pom. Your friends, sir, the hangman. You must be so good, sir,
>   to rise and be put to death.
> Barnardine. [*within.*] Away, you rogue, away; I am sleepy.
> Abhor. Tell him he must awake, and that quickly too.
> Pom. Pray, Master Barnardine, awake till you are executed,
>   and sleep afterwards.

Abhor. Go in to him and fetch him out.
Pom. He is coming, sir, he is coming. I hear his straw rustle.

(IV.iii.21–35)

The situation evoked by this dialogue verifies, on one level, the picture of Barnardine painted by the Provost to the Duke. The shouting needed to wake him confirms a lethargy that has spiritual overtones, while his inability to distinguish his visitors is indicative of the literal and figurative darkness that he inhabits. Abhorson's injunction to Pompey to 'go in to him and fetch him out' has animalistic overtones, while the jailor's reply, 'I hear his straw rustle', supports the implication of a bestial condition. At the same time, Pompey's response to the demand to identify himself ('Your friends, sir, the hangman') reinforces the view propounded by the Duke that release from existence for Barnardine constitutes a benevolent rather than a barbarous act, while the promise of sleep after execution holds out the hope of a more peaceful life for him after death.

While confirming the state of the condemned man projected in the previous scene, however, the interchange between jailor, executioner and prisoner sends out curiously mixed signals, unsettling the audience's conviction of the probity of the Duke's device. In the first place, the scene is a comic one, the stance of Pompey and Abhorson grotesquely at odds with the gravity of their office and the action they are about to perform. The very name 'Abhorson' carries a judgement, implying both the abhorrent and illegitimate nature of the character's office, while the repeated 'rise and be hanged', 'rise and be put to death', associates the condemned man not with a beast but with Christ. The entrance of Barnardine himself, moreover, contributes to the uncertainty of tone. His lack of awareness of the reality of his danger generates alarm for both his physical and his spiritual safety, while his easy familiarity with his jailors permits the audience to view him as a human being, rather than the dehumanized instrument of a theoretically acceptable device.

Enter BARNARDINE.

Abhor. Is the axe upon the block, sirrah?
Pom. Very ready, sir.
Barnardine. How now, Abhorson? What's the news with you?
Abhor. Truly, sir, I would desire you to clap into your
    prayers; for look you, the warrant's come.
Barnardine. You rogue, I have been drinking all night; I
    am not fitted for't.

Pom. O, the better, sir; for he that drinks all night,
and is hanged betimes in the morning, may sleep the
sounder all the next day.

(IV.iii.36–46)

The Duke's entrance in his disguise as a Friar at once heightens concern at the imminence of the execution while carrying the promise of a
return to order and propriety. His tone, once again, is decisive, implying
his control over the situation, while he again offers the hope of spiritual
consolation for the prisoner, if not release from physical danger. It is at
this point in the drama, however, that Shakespeare effects his most sur-
prising overthrow of the expectations generated both by the progress of
the action and the familiarity of the audience with the complex of
stories upon which the interwoven strands of the plot depend. Like
Isabella and Claudio before him, Barnardine refuses point-blank to participate in the course of action designed by others, confounding his
would-be executioners and leaving them wholly at a loss:

> *Enter* DUKE *[disguised]*.
> Abhor. Look you, sir, here comes your ghostly father. Do
> we jest now, think you?
> Duke. Sir, induced by my charity, and hearing how hastily
> you are to depart, I am come to advise you, comfort you,
> and pray with you.
> Barnardine. Friar, not I. I have been drinking hard all
> night, and I will have more time to prepare me, or they
> shall beat out my brains with billets. I will not consent
> to die this day, that's certain.
> Duke. O sir, you must; and therefore I beseech you
> Look forward on the journey you shall go.
> Barnardine. I swear I will not die today for any man's
> persuasion.
> Duke. But hear you –
> Barnardine. Not a word. If you have anything to say to
> me, come to my ward: for thence will not I today.

(IV.iii.47–62)

The stance that Barnardine adopts here, not only frustrates the Duke's
stratagem and the expectations of the theatre audience, it also challenges
the ideological structure in which his society seeks to locate him, making him an object of particular interest to contemporary criticism. The
Duke's position rests upon a set of socio-theological assumptions
embodied both in his own person and in his disguise as a Friar and it is

this set of assumptions that Barnardine resists. In his role as spiritual adviser, and thus as God's representative, the Duke expects to be met with the deference accorded to him by Isabella, Claudio and the Provost, while he seeks to position the execution that he has ordered within a Christian framework. His opening words display his assurance that as a priest, motivated by 'charity',[7] he is able to offer 'advice' and 'comfort' to a condemned man, and that his offer to 'pray' with the prisoner will be welcome. Barnardine's unceremonious 'Friar, not I' not only disables the Duke in his role as spiritual adviser, it also vitiates the propriety of the substitution that he has planned. If Barnardine cannot be brought to the block in a repentant frame of mind, then an act of mercy towards both men under sentence of death is transformed into the reckless endangering of the soul of one man in order to save the life of another, and is no longer consonant with the framework of beliefs in which the power of the Duke resides. At the same time, Barnardine's stance has political as well as spiritual implications in that by refusing to recognize the authority of his would-be head[s]man, Barnardine effectively disempowers him. The confidence that the Duke displays on his first entrance (cf. 'I am come to…') is rapidly eroded in the face of the other's refusal to cooperate with the system upon which his authority depends. In withholding his 'consent' to his own execution, Barnardine thus shifts the balance of power from the Duke to himself, obliging the other to 'beseech' him to allow his death to proceed by viewing the matter in the expected light.

The closing lines of the passage complete the process of reversal effected by the intransigence of the condemned man. Unable by virtue of his own value system to resort to brute force (cf. Barnardine's assertion that 'I will have more time to prepare me or they shall beat out my brains with billets'), the Duke is reduced to persuasion, only to find himself peremptorily interrupted and denied permission to speak (cf. 'Not a word'). Rather than closing, as expected, with the prisoner led away to the block, the episode concludes with Barnardine returning, with the air of a free man, to his own ward, and announcing that the Duke must wait on him, rather than bringing him before him, if he wishes to speak to him again.

---

7. Chief among the Christian virtues as defined by St Paul (cf. *First Epistle to the Corinthians*, 13.13). The term carries the sense of love of one's fellow men, aligning the Duke with the teachings of Christ (cf. 'love thy neighbour as thyself'). The term is thus a potent one in its dramatic context, functioning to legitimate the Duke's conduct towards the prisoner.

The Duke's response to the unexpected conduct of the substitute offering is indicative once again of the impotence of a dominant ideology in the face of a conflicting value system. Barnardine's departure is followed by the entrance of the Provost to whom the Duke reports the failure of the scheme for Claudio's release:

> *Enter* PROVOST.
> Duke. Unfit to live or die! O gravel heart.
> Prov. After him, fellows, bring him to the block!
>   *[Exeunt* ABHORSON *and* POMPEY.
> Now sir, how do you find the prisoner?
> Duke. A creature unprepar'd, unmeet for death;
> And to transport him in the mind he is
> Were damnable.
>
>   (IV.iii.63–8)

The line 'unfit to live or die' sums up Barnardine's position as an outsider in relation to the socio-theological structure represented by the Friar/Duke. As a convicted criminal (i.e. one whose conduct is at variance with the laws of a particular society and the ethical assumptions on which those laws are based), Barnardine is clearly unfit to inhabit the 'Vienna' of the play, yet he is also 'unfit to die' in more than one sense. On the one hand, he is not in the appropriate frame of mind to face judgement in the metaphysical sphere as conceived by the social group, while his ignobility in the eyes of the community makes him incapable of the heroic sacrifice for which he has (unwittingly) been chosen. Moreover, just as Isabella's refusal to yield up her body for Claudio calls in question the integrity of the individual prepared to buy life on such terms, so Barnardine's refusal to die when required to do so reflects back on those in authority over him, and who are bent upon taking his life. The lines 'And to transport him in the mind he is / Were damnable', are highly ambiguous, implying not merely that the prisoner would suffer perdition were he to die in an unrepentant frame of mind, but that those who had obliged him to meet his end in an inappropriate state would be jeopardizing the safety of their own souls.

The alternative version of the tale of the heroic sacrifice enacted in the course of this scene gives way at this point to the canonical process. The Provost recalls that a prisoner (Ragozine), closely resembling Claudio, has died of a fever, and suggests that his head should be sent to Angelo as evidence that the execution that he has ordered has taken place. The Duke embraces the proposal, like his progenitors in the inherited story, as 'an accident that heaven provides' (IV.iii.76), and the head is promptly dispatched to Angelo, permitting the deputy to be entrapped and Claudio saved. What is notable about the sequence of events from Angelo's decision to proceed with the execution after the ransom has supposedly been paid, to the substitution of Ragozine's head for Claudio's by the Duke and Provost, is that Barnardine, for all the fullness of detail surrounding him, is entirely superfluous to the action. Since Ragozine is an acceptable substitute, and Barnardine has no further role in the story (though he does appear in the final scene), the passages involving him have no obvious justification, and could well be cut in the course of performance without apparent detriment to the play. His importance to the scheme of the drama is indicated, however, by the fact that he is the dramatist's own invention, and is entirely without precedent in the sources on which the action is based. Rather than contributing to the evolution of the drama, he functions as the most extreme instance of a number of 'sites of opposition', of voices that interrogate the assumptions encoded in the traditional story, and embodied in the play's authority figures.

As noted above, the tale of Abraham and Isaac quoted at the start of this chapter posits a shared value system that endows the story with a specific meaning. The actors in the Biblical drama function in accordance with a pattern of behaviour predicated upon a particular set of religious beliefs. Abraham recognizes that his prime duty lies towards God rather than a member of his family, and he is willing to sacrifice his son to the deity when required to do so. God, in return, spares the dutiful subject of suffering, while the ram yields up its life on Isaac's behalf. In Shakespeare's alternative version of the story, while the paradigmatic process is constantly evoked, none of the characters conforms to the expected role. From Isabella who places her virginity before her duty to her brother, through Claudio who puts his own life before his sister's welfare, to Angelo who seeks to continue with the execution after the substitute offering has been made, the dramatis personae consistently operate in ways at variance with audience expectation, exhibiting, from one perspective, the corruption of a human society that has fallen away from an implied ideal. The cogency of the positions advanced by the play's oppositional voices, however, frustrate a straightforward reading of the play in homiletic terms. The shared ideology that gives meaning to the inherited story has given place in the Shakespearian drama to a world of conflicting value systems, in which concepts of right conduct do not always coincide. The patriarchal propriety of yielding up her virginity on behalf of her brother is far from clear to Isabella, a prospective bride of Christ,[8] while Claudio cannot readily embrace the proposition that physical dissolution is preferable to what others regard as a dishonoured life. The terms through which the members of the community express their cultural values are consequently destabilized, losing a measure of their universal currency. From Claudio's perspective, for example, Isabella would be performing an act of 'virtue' (cf. III.i.135), were she to submit herself to Angelo, whereas for Isabella the same course of conduct would constitute a 'vice' (III.i.137). Similarly, the sacrifice required of Isabella is not 'heroic' in her eyes but 'foul' (cf. II.iv.113), while the traditional act of self-surrender is not a 'sacrifice' from her viewpoint but a 'rank offence' (III.i.99).

It is through the figure of Barnardine, however, that the subversive character of the play's counter-discourses is most vividly realized. At once the most degenerate character in the drama, and its most potent oppositional voice, he is able to defy the society in which he finds himself in that he endorses none of its terms. Whereas those around him regard prison as a punishment, for example, he is entirely at home in his cell, appropriating as his own domain the quarters to which he has been condemned (cf. 'come to my ward', IV.iii.62), and thus robbing society of a major sanction against him. His drunkenness, deplored by others, is for him a way of life, while from his perspective it is not himself, but Abhorson, who merits description as a 'rogue' (IV.iii.29 and 42) in that he disturbs the peace of the prison and threatens his life. Not only does he act out an alternative version of the tale of the heroic sacrifice by refusing to play the expected part, he inhabits throughout an alternative world in which the assumptions upon which the dominant ideology is founded no longer hold good. Whereas the ram supplied by God in the tale of Abraham and Isaac conforms to a pattern of duties and obligations in being offered in Isaac's place, the bestial scapegoat of *Measure for Measure* has an agenda of his own and, having disengaged himself from his bush of straw, simply walks away. The exhibition of the orderly working of a benign hierarchical universe is thus frustrated, exposing the impotence of a power structure to which the individual denies consent.

Though Barnardine does not speak again after the prison scene of Act IV Scene iii he reappears at the close of the drama when judgement

---

8. The situation of Isabella is a particularly interesting one in relation to Shakespeare's treatment of the inherited story in that she is neither a wife nor a marriageable woman, but a novice in the process of entering a convent. The variation on the source material serves to heighten the clash between conflicting imperatives that Shakespeare's version of the plot sets up.

upon all the characters is passed, his presence serving to expose once again the constructed (rather than inevitable) nature of human institutions. Having engineered the exhibition of Angelo's failings, the Duke requires the remaining prisoners to be brought before him, Barnardine and Angelo thus being brought together for the first time. The characters have stood earlier in the play, at different ends of the moral spectrum, Angelo, as his name implies, the seeming epitome of virtue, Barnardine (as noted above) seen as little more than a beast. Once again the preparation for the latter's appearance is disproportionate to his share of the action, causing the audience to focus upon his entrance at the very moment that Angelo repents of his guilt:

> Duke. I have bethought me of another fault.
> Provost, how came it Claudio was beheaded
> At an unusual hour?
> Prov.   It was commanded so.
> Duke. Had you a special warrant for the deed?
> Prov. No, my good lord: it was by private message.
> Duke. For which I do discharge you of your office.
> Give up your keys.
> Prov.   Pardon me, noble lord;
> I thought it was a fault, but knew it not;
> Yet did repent me after more advice.
> For testimony whereof, one in the prison
> That should by private order else have died,
> I have reserv'd alive.
> Duke.   What's he?
> Prov.   His name is Barnardine.
> Duke. I would thou hadst done so by Claudio.
> Go, fetch him hither, let me look upon him.
>   [*Exit* PROVOST.]
> Esc[alus]. I am sorry one so learned and so wise
> As you, Lord Angelo, have still appear'd,
> Should slip so grossly, both in the heat of the blood
> And lack of temper'd judgement afterward.
> Ang. I am sorry that such sorrow I procure,
> And so deep sticks it in my penitent heart
> That I crave death more willingly than mercy;
> 'Tis my deserving, and I do entreat it.
>
> Enter PROVOST *with* BARNARDINE, CLAUDIO, [*muffled, and*]
>   JULIET.
>
>   (V.i.454–75)

Angelo's words immediately prior to the entrance of the prisoners signal his reassimilation into the society of the play. He accepts the value judgement of the community on his actions, and asks for the appropriate punishment for his sins. His lines, however, are framed by references to Barnardine, inviting the audience to consider the relationship between the attitudes of the two men, and it is to Barnardine that the Duke turns when the prisoners are brought on stage, once again foregrounding a figure essentially superfluous to the plot:

> Duke. Which is that Barnardine?
> Prov.   This, my lord.
> Duke. There was a friar told me of this man.
>   Sirrah, thou art said to have a stubborn soul
>   That apprehends no further than this world,
>   And squar'st thy life according. Thou'rt condemn'd;
>   But, for those earthly faults, I quit them all,
>   And pray thee take this mercy to provide
>   For better times to come. Friar, advise him;
>   I leave him to your hand.
>
>   (V.i.476–84)

A number of points are notable about this scene. In the first place, Shakespeare once again violates the expectations of the audience in relation to the function of the passage. Angelo is in ignorance that Claudio is still alive, and the reintroduction of Barnardine at the moment of the deputy's repentance invites the inference that he is at last to justify his place in the economy of the drama by fulfilling his role as Claudio's substitute in proving not to be Barnardine at all, but the supposedly dead man. In fact, Claudio and Barnardine are brought on stage together, depriving the latter of any role in the process the Duke has engineered, and thus reinforcing audience awareness of his intransigence. At the same time, the judgement that the Duke passes on him is notably different from that exacted upon the remainder of his erring subjects. Whereas the punishments of Angelo, Claudio and Lucio are made to fit their crimes, Barnardine alone is pardoned, and consigned to the care of another Friar. The Duke's sentence reflects his powerlessness in relation to a man whose value system is at variance with that of the social group, while his admonition to the Friar to 'advise' him rings decidedly hollow in the ears of an audience already alerted to the prisoner's imperviousness to instruction. Most significantly of all, Barnardine remains silent to the close of the play, his failure to cooperate in his own trial standing in stark contrast to the conduct of

Angelo who has sought both to exculpate and pass judgement on himself. Where the deputy lends his consent by his conduct to the conceptual framework that both defines his guilt and authorizes his punishment, Barnardine remains aloof from the world of Vienna to the close, his silent presence serving as a continuing reminder of the oppositional stances adopted in the course of the play.

Shakespeare's version of the tale of the heroic sacrifice may be described as an alternative one in more than one respect. No-one behaves in a stereotypically heroic manner, while none of the dramatis personae sacrifices life or honour on another's behalf. Isabella declines to compromise her virtue on behalf of her brother, Claudio exhibits cowardice rather than magnanimous courage, while Barnardine refuses to lay down his life as occasion requires. Nevertheless, the positions adopted by these characters are not without a species of heroism in that they involve resistance to the philosophical framework legitimizing the organization of the social group. Isabella stands against the proposition that the first duty of a woman is to her male relatives; Claudio places his own safety before moral considerations; while Barnardine inverts the value judgements of his world. Moreover, the challenge posed to their society by these figures through their non-conformist attitudes is singularly potent. Since Isabella rejects the assumptions that would justify her sacrificing her honour on behalf of her brother, Claudio has no means of requiring her to do so, and is left with no recourse but (ineffective) persuasion, and the same applies to the Duke in his dealings with Barnardine. Where the traditional tale of the heroic sacrifice exhibits the harmonious operation of a divinely ordained hierarchical system, Shakespeare's alternative version reveals that political power depends on consent, and that it collapses when that consent is withheld. It is interesting to note, given the current debate over the dramatist's political stance, that the earliest recorded reference to *Measure for Measure* is to a performance at court in 1604 – the year following the accession of a monarch prepared to countenance a greater degree of reflection than his immediate predecessor on the mystique of royalty.[9]

The elaborate game of heads that is played in Shakespeare's version of the tale of the heroic sacrifice is not without its modern equivalents. Angelo demands a maidenhead to avert a beheading, while the Duke orders a beheading to save a head. Those caught up in others' machinations resist the impositions, refusing to pay the price their superiors demand. Of the voices raised in opposition, Barnardine's is at once the most absolute and the most efficacious, in that he exposes that those in authority cannot rule, without resorting to violent means, if the consent of the subject is withheld. Faced with a poll tax of the most literal kind, Barnardine responds, like his 1990s counterparts resisting a rather less lethal impost, with an uncompromising 'Friar, not I', forcing the Duke into an embarrassing u-turn. Cast as the dutiful ram lodged in the bush, he reinvents his own role, revealing the vulnerability of all political institutions with the seventeenth-century equivalent of 'Can't pay, won't pay'.

Chapter 5

All's Well That Ends Well and the Tale of the Chivalric Quest

His joyful mariners ... spread forth their comely sails, and with their brazen keels cut an easy passage on the green meadows of the floods. At last, Fortune having brought him here where she might make him the fittest tennis ball for her sport.... the heavens began to thunder, and the skies shone with flashes of fire; day now had no other show but only name, for darkness was on the whole face of the waters ... And partly through that dismal darkness, which unfortunately was come upon them, they were all drowned, [the prince] only excepted, till (as it were Fortune being tired with this mishap) by the help of a plank, which in this distress he got hold on, he was with much labour and more fear driven on the shore.... Certain fishermen, who had also suffered in the former tempest, and had been witness of his untimely shipwreck, the day being cleared again, were come out of their homely cottages to dry and repair their nets.... The chief of these fishermen was moved with compassion toward him, and lifting him up from the ground himself, with the help of his men led him to his house.... Being somewhat repaired in heart by their relief, he demanded of the country on which he was driven, of the name of the king.... and then how far his court was distant from that place, wherein he was resolved some half a day's journey, and from point to point also informed that the king had a princely daughter ... in whom was beauty so joined with virtue that it was as yet unresolved which of them deserved the greater comparison, and in memory of whose birthday her father yearly celebrated feasts and triumphs, in the honour of which many princes and knights from far and remote countries came, partly to prove their chivalry, but especially (being her father's only child) in hope to gain her love ... [The prince], sighing to himself ... broke out thus, 'Were but my fortunes answerable to my desires, some should feel that I would be one there.' When, as if all the gods had given a plaudite to his words, the fishermen who before were sent out by their master to drag out the other nets, having found somewhat in the bottom too ponderous for their strength to pull up, they began to ... halloo to their master for more help ... [but] before help came, up came the fish expected, but proved indeed to be a rusty armour ... The armour is by [the prince] viewed, and known to be a defence which his father at his last will gave him in charge to keep, that it might prove to be a defender of the son, which he had known to be a preserver of the father. So, accounting all his other losses nothing ... and thanking Fortune that after all her crosses she had yet given him somewhat to repair his fortunes, begging this armour of the fishermen [he told them] that with it he would show the virtue he had learned in arms, and try his chivalry for their princess ... Which they applauding, and one furnishing him with an old gown to make caparisons for his horse ... and other furnishing him with the long sideskirts of their cassocks to make him bases,[1] his armour rusted and thus disgracefully habilited, [the prince] ... came to the court. In this manner also, five several princes, their horses richly caparisoned, but themselves more richly armed, their pages before them bearing their devices on their shields, entered then the tilting place ... The sixth and last was [the prince] who, having neither page to deliver his shield, nor shield to deliver, making his device according to his fortunes, which was a withered branch being only green at the top, which proved the abating of his body decayed not the nobleness of his mind, his word,[2] *In hac spe vivo*.... The peers attending on the king forbore not to scoff, both at his presence and the present he bought ... which the king mildly reproving them for, he told them that as virtue was not to be proved by words, but by actions, so the outward habit was the least table of the inward mind ... They went forward to the triumph, in which noble exercise they came almost all as short of [the prince] ... as a body dying of a life flourishing. To be short, both of court and commons, the praises of none were spoken of but of the mean knight's ... The triumphs being ended, [the prince] as chief (for in this day's honour he was the champion) with all the other princes were ... conducted into the presence ... at whose entrance the lady, first saluting [him] gave him a wreath of chivalry, welcomed him as her knight and guest, and crowned him king of that day's noble enterprise ... Both king and daughter, at one instant were so struck in love with the nobleness of his worth, that they could not spare so much time to satisfy themselves with the delicacy of their viands for talking of his praises ... At last, the father, being no longer able to subdue that which he desired as much as she ... clapped them hand in hand, while they as lovingly joined lip to lip, and with tears trickling from his aged eyes, adopted him his happy son, and bad them live together as man and wife.

(George Wilkins, *The Painful Adventures of Pericles Prince of Tyre*, 1608)[3]

---

1. A cloth skirt, usually of rich material, attached to the doublet and extending from waist to knee.
2. i.e. motto.
3. Based upon the text in Kenneth Muir (ed.) (1967) *The Painfull Aduentures of Pericles Prince of Tyre*, Liverpool University Press, but with modernized spelling and punctuation. The extracts quoted are from ch. 4 but for the closing sentence which is drawn from ch. 6.

The story of the chivalric quest, exemplified by George Wilkins' tale of the shipwrecked prince, combines a number of very ancient folk tale motifs. At the heart of the story lies the concept of life as a journey,[4] with storm representing the vicissitudes to which all human beings are subject. The motif is a common one throughout western European literature, and is found in the vernacular English tradition as early as the Anglo-Saxon period in such poems as *The Seafarer*. At the same time the story also has its roots in the fertility myths, common to many cultures, in which the health of a society is seen as dependent upon the virility of its ruler. In Wilkins' story the aging king has no son to succeed him, and the ritual combats between those seeking to achieve his daughter's hand ensure that the heir to the kingdom will marry a husband capable of maintaining the health of the state. Once again, the story enjoyed wide currency during the Middle Ages, flourishing both in the form of a heroic deed on behalf of a lady (looking back to such classical myths as that of Perseus and Andromeda), and as a quest to rejuvenate a waste land ruled over by a stricken king (cf. the legend of the holy grail).

A common feature of many of the items making up this complex of tales is the prowess or supreme virtue of a person of seemingly low rank. Just as Wilkins' destitute prince is scorned by his fellow combatants for his mean appearance, but proves his valour and wins the princess's love, so Sir Gareth (ultimately one of the most celebrated of the knights of the round table) begins his career as a kitchen boy despised by Sir Kay, but exhibits his knightly virtue in the performance of a quest, marries the lady of Lyoness and is revealed to be the son of a king.[5] As in Wilkins' tale, moreover, the fulfilment of the hero's destiny is frequently accomplished, both in romance and classical fable, by means of an object of particular value inherited from a father, or provided by supernatural powers. Hercules, for example, a son of Zeus, receives arms and armour from the gods, while Sir Galahad, who comes to Arthur's court without weapons, is magically provided with a sword and shield.

The density of meaning afforded by the overlap between strands within this nexus of stories is exhibited by Spenser's *The Faerie Queene* (1590 and 1596). Like Wilkins' narrative, the poem draws together a number of familiar elements, firmly locating the work in a literary tradition. The central figures of Book I, a knight and a lady, are first

---

4. Sometimes referred to as the *peregrinatio* (Latin, 'travel') motif.
5. Compare the story of Sir Perceval who also emerges from humble origins to become one of the foremost of Arthur's knights.

encountered in the course of a journey; the knight is of mean appearance (in that his armour is battered and old), while the lady is in need of help. The knight's identity is uncertain, and he discovers his destiny in the course of his mission to slay a dragon, restore the stricken land of his companion's parents and thus win the lady herself as his bride. While the elements of the story clearly correspond to those of Wilkins' narrative, however, the significance the poem is much more profound. Spenser's work is an allegory, marrying folk tale and chivalric romance to Christian teaching, and thus endowing the strands of the inherited fable with a new richness. The Redcross Knight is not simply mankind engaged upon the eventful journey through life, or the embodiment of a life-force dispelling winter and bringing new growth, he is a Christian everyman seeking to overcome evil and perfect himself, emulating the conduct of Christ in reversing the fall. His battered armour is not merely a physical inheritance derived from an earthly father, but the gift of God in the form of his word (cf. St Paul's injunction to the Ephesians to 'take unto you the whole armour of God'), while the wasteland awaiting its saviour is not only a land gripped by winter but the post-lapsarian world. The reader of the poem thus engages with the knight's adventures on a number of levels, each incident carrying a range of resonances by virtue of the fusion effected between different traditions.

At first sight, *All's Well That Ends Well* has little in common with the type of story exemplified by Wilkins' tale. The plot of the play is derived from Boccaccio's *Decameron* (Day 3, Story 9) mediated, in all probability, through William Painter's sixteenth-century anthology, *The Palace of Pleasure* (Story 38)[6]. Rather than concerning the deeds of a knight or the winning of a lady, Boccaccio's story is centred upon the career of a physician's daughter (Gilette of Narbonne) and her pursuit of the young Count of Roussillon, son of her father's former patron. Being of lower rank than the man she loves, Gilette has no hope of being his bride, until on hearing that the King is suffering from an illness, she attends the court and effects his cure, asking for the hand of the Count (a ward of the King) as her reward. The King reluctantly complies with her request, and Gilette returns home to manage her husband's estates, but the Count refuses to consummate the marriage, requiring his virgin bride to bear his child and to produce a ring he values from his finger before he will accept her as his wife. Faced with such seemingly impossible conditions, and fearing her presence at Rousillon is barring the

---

6. First published in 1566 and expanded in 1567 and 1575.

Count from returning home, Gilette undertakes a pilgrimage to Florence, only to learn upon her arrival that her husband is engaged there upon the seduction of another woman. Seeing an opportunity to fulfil his conditions, Gilette persuades the other lady to demand the Count's ring as the price of her compliance, and to allow her to take her place in her husband's bedchamber. Having become pregnant with twins after a number of encounters, Gilette presents herself before the Count with the ring and not one but two children and is gladly received by him as his wife.

Though heavily reliant upon folk tale, Boccaccio's story clearly derives from a different tradition from that to which Wilkins' narrative belongs. Gilette's experience looks back to the fable of the long-suffering wife (cf. Chaucer's *The Clerk's Tale* and Renaissance plays such as John Phillip's *Patient and Meek Grissil*, 1558–61), while the conditions imposed by her husband belong to 'the tale of impossibilities', and the achievement of a seemingly unattainable goal.[7] In taking up Painter's version of Boccaccio's story, however, Shakespeare fuses the borrowed material with elements from a different literary stock (cf. Spenser's treatment of the chivalric quest in *The Fairie Queene*), interrogating the assumptions underlying his inherited stories through the interaction that he sets up between them.

Though broadly comparable with the situation of Boccaccio's heroine, Helena's position at the opening of *All's Well That Ends Well* differs from that of her romance progenitor in a number of respects. Gilette, like Painter's Giletta, conceives a passion for the young Count at a very early age, and there is a hint of impropriety in the degree of her infatuation with him. Boccaccio describes her as 'more passionately attached to him than was strictly proper in a girl of so tender an age',[8] while Painter notes that she 'fervently fell in love with Beltramo, more than was meet for a maiden'.[9] Shakespeare's heroine, by contrast, is

7. For a fuller discussion of the folk tale motifs brought together in *All's Well That Ends Well*, see Geoffrey Bullough (1957–75), *Narrative and Dramatic Sources of Shakespeare*, vol.ii, Routledge and Kegan Paul, pp. 375ff; W.W. Lawrence (1931) *Shakespeare's Problem Comedies*, Penguin Shakespeare Library edition, 1969, pp. 48ff; and my (1992) *Shakespeare's Mouldy Tales*, Longman, pp. 100ff.
8. Quoted from G.H. McWilliam (ed.) (1972) *The Decameron*, Penguin Classics, p. 305. All subsequent references to Boccaccio's work are to this edition.
9. Quoted from the 1575 edition in Bullough, *Narrative and Dramatic Sources of Shakespeare*, vol.ii, p. 389 but with modernized spelling and punctuation. All subsequent references to Painter's story are to this edition.

noted for her virtue from the outset, the lines in which she is introduced
to the audience placing particular emphasis upon her purity of mind:

> Laf[ew]. Was this gentlewoman the daughter of Gerard de Narbon?
> Count[ess]. His sole child, my lord, and bequeathed to my
> overlooking. I have those hopes of her good that her
> education promises her dispositions she inherits – which
> makes fair gifts fairer; for where an unclean mind carries
> virtuous qualities, there commendations go with pity; they
> are virtues and traitors too. In her they are the better for
> their simpleness: she derives her honesty and achieves her
> goodness.
>
> (I.i.33–42)

The heroine's social position has also undergone a notable change
between prose works and play. Gilette is the daughter of a very wealthy
man, and the latter's kinsmen are concerned to ensure that his daughter
should make an appropriate marriage after his death. Boccaccio emphasizes that Gilette 'had inherited the whole of her father's fortune', that
she was 'kept under constant surveillance' and that 'after reaching marriageable age' because of her love of the young Count she 'rejected
numerous suitors whom her kinsfolk had urged her to marry' (p. 305).
Similarly Painter's Giletta was 'diligently looked unto by her kinsfolk
(because she was rich and fatherless) ... and refused many husbands with
whom her kinsfolk would have matched her' (pp. 389–90). Helena by
contrast is a 'poor physician's daughter' (II.iii.123), friendless but for her
patroness, the Countess,[10] and thus at a far greater social distance from
the man she hopes to attain than the figures from whom she derives.
Where both Gilette and Giletta have independent means, Helena is a
dependent of the Count's household, her position heightening the
improbability of her achieving her goal. At the same time, the circumstances surrounding the relationship between the heroine's father and
the former Count of Rousillon (Shakespeare's Rossillion) has also been
significantly adapted between source and play. Boccaccio's old Count is
described as 'something of an invalid' (p. 305) requiring the constant
attendance of a physician, while Painter's nobleman is more
emphatically 'sickly and diseased', obliged to keep a doctor 'always in
his house' (p. 389). Shakespeare's Count, by contrast, was an outstanding individual in both physical and mental terms, his exceptional gifts
vividly evoked for the audience through the words of the King:

---

10. Her 'poor, but honest' friends (I.iii.190) are referred to in the past tense.

> I would I had that corporal soundness now,
> As when thy father [i.e.the young Count's] and myself in friendship
> First tried our soldiership. He did look far
> Into the service of the time, and was
> Discipled of the bravest. He lasted long,
> But on us both did haggish age steal on,
> And wore us out of act. It much repairs me
> To talk of your good father; in his youth
> He had the wit which I can well observe
> Today in our young lords; but they may jest
> Till their own scorn return to them unnoted
> Ere they can hide their levity in honour.
> So like a courtier, contempt nor bitterness
> Were in his pride or sharpness; if they were,
> His equal had awak'd them, and his honour,
> Clock to itself, knew the true minute when
> Exception bid him speak, and at this time
> His tongue obey'd his hand. Who were below him
> He us'd as creatures of another place,
> And bow'd his eminent top to their low ranks,
> Making them proud of his humility
> In their poor praise he humbled. Such a man
> Might be a copy to these younger times;
> Which, followed well, would demonstrate them now
> But goers backward.

(I.ii.24–48)

The King's eulogy of the former Count, while establishing the exemplary nature of the dead man, also serves to associate his virtues with those of an old order. His nobility of mind and vigour of body are linked with the condition of the state in that he and the King were bound together in 'friendship', enjoyed a similar 'corporal soundness', and 'tried [their] soldiership' together. The eminent physician associated with the Count's family is thus not a necessary prop to a decayed household, but a further instance of the excellence of an earlier age when both the military and social arts flourished. The demise of the old Count, together with the King's illness and the death of Helena's father consequently suggest the decay of an entire society, a point emphasized by the King's comparison between the limited capacities of the younger members of his court and the qualities of his former friend.

The King's response to the reward that the heroine asks in return for the cure that she effects is also indicative of the different shape that

Shakespeare imposes on his inherited narrative. Boccaccio's King, having agreed to permit Gilette to marry the man of her choice, is disturbed when she asks for the Count of Roussillon for 'it was no laughing matter to [him] that he should be obliged to give her Bertrand' (p. 307). Similarly, Painter's sick ruler agrees to Giletta's conditions, but when appraised of her choice of husband is 'very loath to grant him unto her' (p. 391). The hesitation on the part of both monarchs contributes to the sense of impropriety surrounding the early stages of the heroine's career, while providing implicit justification for the Count's refusal to accept his low-born wife. Shakespeare's King by contrast has no hesitation in granting Helena's request, rebuking the reluctant Bertram for the false values that he exhibits in repudiating the match:

> 'Tis only title thou disdain'st in her, the which
> I can build up. Strange is it that our bloods,
> Of colour, weight, and heat, pour'd all together,
> Would quite confound distinction, yet stands off
> In differences so mighty. If she be
> All that is virtuous, save what thou dislik'st –
> A poor physician's daughter – thou dislik'st
> Of virtue for the name. But do not so.
> From lowest place when virtuous things proceed,
> The place is dignified by th'doer's deed.
> Where great additions swell's and virtue none,
> It is a dropsied honour. Good alone
> Is good, without a name; vileness is so:
> The property by what it is should go,
> Not by the title. She is young, wise, fair;
> In these to nature she's immediate heir,
> And these breed honour; that is honour's scorn
> Which challenges itself as honour's born
> And is not like the sire. Honours thrive
> When rather from our acts we them derive
> Than our forgoers. The mere word's a slave,
> Debosh'd on every tomb, on every grave
> A lying trophy, and as oft is dumb,
> Where dust and damn'd oblivion is the tomb
> Of honour'd bones indeed. What should be said?
> If thou canst like this creature as a maid,
> I can create the rest. Virtue and she
> Is her own dower; honour and wealth from me.

(II.iii.117–44)

The King's stance contributes to the contrast established by the
dramatist between the true nobility of an old order and the corruption
of a new age, and this contrast is heightened by Shakespeare's introduction of an old courtier, Lafew, who endorses the King's position. While
Bertram exclaims that he 'cannot love her nor will strive to do't'
(II.iii.145), Lafew regrets that he cannot be among those from whom
Helena is to make her choice (II.iii.78–9), and is horrified by the attitude of the younger lords towards her:

> Do all they deny her? And they were sons of mine I'd
> have them whipp'd, or I would send them to th'Turk
> to make eunuchs of.

> (II.iii.86–8)

While heightening the contrast between the former condition of
society and the decayed nature of the world in which the miraculous
cure is to be effected, Shakespeare also draws much greater attention
than the sources on which he draws to the difficulties of the journey
that his central figure undergoes. Boccaccio's Gilette, a wealthy woman,
simply learns of the King's illness, prepares 'certain herbs' and 'rode off
to Paris' (pp. 305–6), while Painter's Giletta 'made a powder of certain
herbs which she thought meet for that disease, and rode to [the capital]'
(p. 390). Helena, by contrast, initially conceives of winning Bertram
through curing the King at the close of the first scene, but fails to act
upon her plan until after the young Count's arrival at court (Scene ii).
Rather than being free to act as she pleases, she is dependent upon her
patroness, the Countess, and the difficulties that her project poses are
emphasized by the stress laid by the latter upon the improbability of her
gaining the King's ear, and on the means that the older woman provides
to enable her to undertake the journey:

> Count. But think you, Helen,
>   If you should tender your supposed aid,
>   He would receive it? He and his physicians
>   Are of a mind; he, that they cannot help him;
>   They, that they cannot help. How shall they credit
>   A poor unlearned virgin, when the schools,
>   Embowel'd of their doctrine, have left off
>   The danger to itself?
> Hel.   There's something in't
>   More than my father's skill, which was the great'st
>   Of his profession, that his good receipt
>   Shall for my legacy be sanctified

By th'luckiest stars in heaven; and would your honour
But give me leave to try success, I'd venture
The well-lost life of mine on his grace's cure
By such a day, an hour.
...
Count. Why, Helen, thou shalt have my leave and love,
Means and attendants, and my loving greetings
To those of mine at court. I'll stay at home
And pray God's blessing into thy attempt.
Be gone tomorrow; and be sure of this,
What I can help thee to, thou shalt not miss.

(I.iii.230–51)

The adaptations made by Shakespeare to his source material clearly serve to move his story away from one designed to exhibit the way in which individuals may 'by dint of their own efforts [achieve] an object they greatly desired' (*Decameron*, p. 231) towards a very different literary tradition. The drama welds the tale of the enterprising woman to that group of stories concerned with the exemplary worth of a person of humble origins, who journeys to regenerate a stricken kingdom through an inheritance of mysterious potency, and is rewarded with marriage to one of higher rank. That Shakespeare was consciously imposing the pattern of the chivalric quest upon his inherited material is indicated, moreover, by an exchange between the Countess and her Steward in I.iii. Having overheard Helena confess her love for Bertram, the Steward conveys the news to his mistress, the terminology in which he does so serving to locate the heroine's conduct in a very different arena from that evoked by the source:

Stew. Madam, I was very late more near her than I think
she wish'd me; alone she was and did communicate to herself
her own words to her own ears ... Her matter was, she loved
your son. Fortune, she said, was no goddess, that had put
such difference betwixt their two estates; Love no god, that
would not extend his might only where qualities were level;
[Diana no] queen of virgins, that would suffer her poor knight
surpris'd without rescue in the first assault or ransom
afterward.

(I.iii.102–12)

While the fusion with a different tradition expands the resonance of Boccaccio's story, the transference of the tale of the heroic quest into the formula supplied by the *Decameron* affords an alternative version or mirror image of the chivalric story. The traditional tale is concerned with the exhibition of masculine virtue, and takes place within the male arena. As in Wilkins' narrative, the central figure is a prince or knight, who proves his virtue in physical combat and wins a passive and admiring bride. By adapting Boccaccio's story into conformity with this pattern, Shakespeare reverses the terms of the inherited tale. His central figure is not a youthful knight attempting to prove his worth and win a bride, but a young woman in pursuit of a husband, while those that support her endeavours are not the conventional embodiments of the chivalric ideal (e.g. the members of King Arthur's court), but female figures traditionally hostile to virtue (a mother-in-law and a widow).[11] Rather than being written from the perspective of a male protagonist, the play thus encourages audience alignment with the female point of view, the implication of impropriety in Boccaccio's narrative functioning as a springboard for an exploration of the assumptions governing gender behaviour encoded within the traditional story.

Where Wilkins' tale centres firmly upon the travels and experience of a prince, Shakespeare's alternative version of the chivalric story begins in the domestic, and thus implicitly female, sphere. The opening lines of the play are unique in the Shakespearian canon in that they are spoken by a woman,[12] while the absence of male authority at Rossillion is indicated by the fact that the speaker is in mourning for her husband and is in process of yielding up her son to the guardianship of the King. The opening conversation, moreover, rather than centring upon the character of the young Count, swiftly shifts to Helena's outstanding virtue. While Bertram is largely a spectator to the conversation between Lafew and his mother, and thus plays a traditionally female role, the Countess's gentlewoman is quickly foregrounded by a reference to her parentage, and it is her situation which is then revealed, through soliloquy, when the other characters leave the stage. Though she is then joined by Parolles, the remainder of the scene is concerned, not with the expectations of the men leaving for Paris, but with male attitudes to women and Helena's state of mind, concluding with a soliloquy that reveals a mental cast wholly at odds with the marginalized role in which the

---

11. For a fuller discussion of the first of these figures see below, pp. 119ff. Whereas both the Countess and the Widow who comes to Helena's aid in the close of Act III are known for their virtue, widows are generally noted for their lack of sexual restraint on the Renaissance stage (cf. Marston's *The Insatiate Countess*, c.1610–13).

12. The first lines of *Macbeth* are spoken by the Witches, but as bearded creatures who 'look not like th'inhabitants o'th'earth' (I.iii.41) their sexual nature is ambiguous.

young Count seeks to cast her (cf. 'Be comfortable to my mother, your mistress, and make much of her', I.i.73–4):

> Hel.   Our remedies oft in ourselves do lie,
>   Which we ascribe to heaven; the fated sky
>   Gives us free scope; only doth backward pull
>   Our slow designs when we ourselves are dull.
>   What power is it which mounts my love so high,
>   That makes me see, and cannot feed mine eye?
>   The mightiest space in fortune nature brings
>   To join like likes, and kiss like native things.
>   Impossible be strange attempts to those
>   That weigh their pains in sense, and do suppose
>   What hath been cannot be. Who ever strove
>   To show her merit that did miss her love?
>   The king's disease – my project may deceive me,
>   But my intents are fix'd, and will not leave me.
>
>   (I.i.212–25)

While this speech would be unexceptionable in the mouth of a man, indicating nobility of mind and steadfastness of purpose, it is not one that fits comfortably with Renaissance assumptions about the nature of women and their social role. As recent criticism has demonstrated,[13] female figures on the Elizabethan-Jacobean stage tend to fall into three classes – virgin, whore and witch – and though Helena clearly belongs in physical terms to the first category, she betrays none of the retiring character generally associated with that figure. While Bertram plays a passive, and hence stereoptypically female, part, in that he is removed from the custody of his mother into the guardianship of the King, who assigns him a marital partner and forbids him to go to the wars, Helena actively pursues the husband of her choice, and plans to leave the shelter of the Countess's protection in order to seek her fortunes in the larger world. Though she clearly corresponds to Boccaccio's Gillete, more-over, in 'being more passionately attached' to Bertram than conventionally 'proper' for a girl of her age, it is clear from the opening exchanges that in the world of *All's Well That Ends Well* female tenacity of purpose is in no way an index of moral failure. Placed in the context of a mind which 'derives [its] honesty and achieves [its] goodness' (I.i.42), the heterodox attitudes that Helena exhibits serve to redefine feminine virtue, setting up a tension between the stances adopted by the

13. See, for example, Jeanne Addison French (1991) *The Shakespearean Wild: Geography, Genus, Gender*, University of Nebraska Press, *passim*.

characters and the expectations generated by the inherited pattern to which the action of the drama conforms.

The reversal of gender expectations effected in I.i. is sustained in the remainder of the act. Though the second scene is set in the court and is dominated by the King it occupies only seventy-five lines (largely devoted to evoking the decayed nature of the play world), and Bertram's role (consisting of only seven lines) is again a minor one. Rather than establishing the youthful Count's heroic resolution, the scene reinforces his dependency, closing with him being 'comfortable' to the King in lending him his arm (I.ii.73), and thus playing the role he assigned to Helena. Scene iii, by contrast, which returns to Rossillion, is the longest of the act, and focuses almost exclusively on female figures. The scene is dominated by the Countess and her opening line, 'I will now hear. What say you of this gentlewoman?' (I.iii.1) serves both to establish her authority and confirm the interest in female concerns. The firmness of tone with which she addresses those about her (cf. 'What does this knave here?', I.iii.7; 'Get you gone, sir; I'll talk with you more anon': I.iii.62) is in sharp contrast to the elegiac style adopted by the King (cf. 'Since I nor wax nor honey can bring home, / [I wish] I ... were dissolved from my hive / To give some labourers room', I.ii.65–7), while the deference exhibited towards her by her male servants confirms her ability to govern (cf. 'May it please you, madam', I.iii.63). The Clown's comment, 'that man should be at woman's command, and yet no hurt done' (I.iii.89–90) draws the attention of the audience towards the play's reversal of roles, while confirming the positive nature of the transgressive stances that the female characters adopt.

The second half of the scene widens the discrepancy between the expectations generated by the play's pattern and the positions that the dramatis personae assume. The Steward reveals to the Countess that her protégé is in love with, and dreams of marrying, her son, and the older woman responds by commanding the younger to be brought before her. A host of literary conventions invites the audience to expect a violent confrontation to ensue between the two women. The Countess's role in relation to Helena is analogous to that of a stepmother, and indeed she refers to herself in these terms (cf. 'You ne'er oppress'd me with a mother's groan / Yet I express to you a mother's care' (I.iii.142–3), encouraging the audience to equate her with the malign step-dames of folk tale inveterately hostile to those in their charge (cf. *Snow White*).[14] At

---

14. See also the vicious Queen in Shakespeare's *Cymbeline* for a typical example of this figure.

the same time, the exclusivity of the Countess's relationship with Bertram, as a widow with an only son, invites the assumption of maternal possessiveness (cf. the stereotype of the embittered mother-in-law), while the stress upon the discrepancy between Helena's station and that of the man she presumes to love touches upon tales of maternal pride. The initial exchange between the two women, moreover, appears to confirm audience expectation. In seeking to evade a definition of her relationship with the Countess that would make her Bertram's sister, Helena betrays the cause of her grief at the Count's departure, producing a seemingly hostile response from her mistress;

> Hel. You are my mother, madam; would you were –
>   So that my lord your son were not my brother –
>   Indeed my mother! or were you both our mothers
>   I care no more for than I do for heaven,
>   So I were not his sister. Can't no other
>   But, I your daughter, he must be my brother?
> Count. Yes, Helen, you might be my daughter-in-law.
>   God shield you mean it not! daughter and mother
>   So strive upon your pulse. What! pale again?
>   My fear hath catch'd your fondness; now I see
>   The myst'ry of your loneliness, and find
>   Your salt tears' head. Now to all sense 'tis gross:
>   You love my son. Invention is asham'd
>   Against the proclamation of thy passion
>   To say thou dost not. Therefore tell me true;
>   But tell me then, 'tis so; for, look, thy cheeks
>   Confess it t'one to th'other, and thine eyes
>   See it so grossly shown in thy behaviours
>   That in their kind they speak it; only sin
>   And hellish obstinacy tie thy tongue,
>   That truth should be suspected. Speak, is't so?
>   If it be so, you have wound a goodly clew;
>   If it be not, forswear't; howe'er, I charge thee,
>   As heaven shall work in me for thine avail,
>   To tell me truly.
> Hel.   Good madam, pardon me.
> Count. Do you love my son?
> Hel.   Your pardon, noble mistress.
> Count. Love you my son?
> Hel.   Do not you love him, madam?
> Count. Go not about; my love hath in't a bond
>   Whereof the world takes note. Come, come, disclose

> The state of your affection, for your passions
> Have to the full appeach'd.
> Hel.   Then I confess,
> Here on my knee, before high heaven and you,
> That before you, and next unto high heaven,
> I love your son.
>
>   (I.iii.156–89)

In the event, however, the conduct of the Countess is at the opposite extreme from that of the conventional 'hag'. Having forced a confession of love from the younger woman, she facilitates rather than opposes the socially unequal marriage between her 'gentlewoman' and her son, enabling Helena to travel to Paris, and thus to prosecute her plans. Rather than being blinded by affection for Bertram, she is keenly aware of her protégé's worth, becoming increasingly convinced as the action progresses not that her son is too good for Helena, but that the Count's conduct shows him to be wholly 'unworthy' of such a wife (III.iv.26).

While the sympathetic presentation of the assertive women of Act I serves to subvert gender stereotypes, the events of Act II call in question the assumptions governing the roles that women are conventionally assigned. In a reversal of the traditional pattern of the chivalric story, the inexperienced virgin (cf. the untried squire) emerges from her obscure condition and travels to the Court, winning the approbation of the King in curing his illness. Where the young knight of the conventional tale wins a bride (cf. Wilkins' princess) as a reward for his valour, Helena asks for a husband as the prize for her attempt, and is promised the reward that she seeks. The scene that follows traditionally constitutes the climactic moment of the inherited story representing the turning point in a cycle of decay and renewal, and thus an occasion of joy. The young knight is united in marriage with the bride whom he has won, symbolizing both the sanctity and fertility of the new order. Shakespeare's alternative version of this culminatory moment is productive, however, of a very different effect. Rather than generating a sense of happiness and propriety, the scene sends out contradictory signals, undermining the acquiescence of the spectator in the events that are taking place.

Whereas in Wilkins' narrative the principal participants in the betrothment ritual are in emotional accord with one another, in the Shakespearian version of the story a marked tension exists between the attitudes of those caught up in the play's events. Unlike Boccaccio's newly healed monarch, who finds Gilette's choice of husband 'no laughing matter' and acquaints the young man in private with the marriage he must make, the King exhibits no sign of disquiet at the prospect of keeping his promise, requiring his young lords to be brought before him, and ceremonially inviting his benefactress to make her choice among his wards:

> King. Go, call before me all the lords in court.
> > [*Exit Attendant.*]
> Sit, my preserver, by thy patient's side,
> And with this healthful hand, whose banish'd sense
> Thou hast repeal'd, a second time receive
> The confirmation of my promis'd gift,
> Which but attends thy naming.
> > *Enter three or four lords.*
> Fair maid, send forth thine eye. This youthful parcel
> Of noble bachelors stand at my bestowing,
> O'er whom both sovereign power and father's voice
> I have to use. Thy frank election make;
> Thou hast power to choose, and they none to forsake.
> ...
> > Peruse them well.
> Not one of those but had a noble father.
>
> > > (II.iii.46–62)

The King's stance enforces the propriety of the situation, and its rightness is confirmed on one level by the sense of recognition that the stage spectacle itself evokes. The scene set up by the dramatist is not only a familiar one in chivalric literature, it was acted out until modern times on every dance floor, with a member of a privileged social group making a choice of partner among a gathering of the opposite sex. Where the scene differs from both social and literary norms, however, and thus challenges audience acceptance, is in its reversal of traditional roles. Whereas men are conventionally the active agents in the mating process and women the passive objects of their election, here it is a female character who is in a position to exercise freedom of choice and the male members of society who are obliged to defer to her will. While the King, moreover, is entirely at ease with the situation, the elderly Lafew assumes that his subjects resent their imposed parts (II.iii.86–8), while Helena herself betrays an embarrassment that invites the spectator to assess her conduct against cultural norms:

Hel. I am a simple maid, and therein wealthiest
    That I protest I simply am a maid.
    Please it your majesty, I have done already.
    The blushes in my cheeks thus whisper me:
    'We blush that thou should'st choose; but, be refused,
    Let the white death sit on thy cheek for ever,
    We'll ne'er come there again'.

(II.iii.66–72)

It is Bertram's response to the situation, however, which is most plainly at odds with the joyous harmony evoked by the scene's romance antecedents, crystallizing the growing unease of those outside the play world. Rather than consenting to be given in marriage like his female counterparts in the inherited story, the young Count furiously repudiates the process in which he has been obliged to participate, vigorously maintaining his right to choose his partner in marriage for himself:

Hel. [*To Bertram*] I dare not say I take you, but I give
    Me and my service, ever whilst I live,
    Into your guiding power. This is the man.
King. Why, then, young Bertram, take her; she's thy wife.
Ber. My wife, my liege! I shall beseech your highness,
    In such a business give me leave to use
    The help of mine own eyes.
King.   Know'st thou not, Bertram,
    What she has done for me?
Ber.   Yes, my good lord,
    But never hope to know why I should marry her.
King. Thou know'st she has rais'd me from my sickly bed.
Ber. But follows it, my lord, to bring me down
    Must answer for your raising? I know her well:
    She had her breeding at my father's charge –
    A poor physician's daughter my wife! Disdain
    Rather corrupt me ever!

(II.iii.102–16)

On one level, Bertram's response to his situation clearly invites audience condemnation. As the King's ward and feudal subject he owes him absolute obedience and the tone in which he addresses him is plainly deficient in respect (cf. 'But follows it, my lord, to bring me down / Must answer for your raising?'). His objection to Helena is founded not upon any inadequacies of character or person, but upon the lowliness of her rank, betraying an unthinking snobbery that contrasts unfavourably with his parents' magnanimity (cf. I.ii.41–5 and I.iii.246–51). At the same time, however, the position that he adopts, for all the unfortunate tone in which it is couched, is not entirely devoid of appeal. The situation in which he finds himself is a demeaning one in terms of the conventional relations between the sexes, while his contention that he has a right to be consulted on a subject upon which his future happiness depends is a sympathetic one, carrying weight in the context of a drama in which the principal characters are motivated by love (cf. Helena and the Countess) rather than pragmatic considerations.

It is not solely the divergent responses of the dramatis personae and consequent division of audience sympathy, however, that serves to problematize the interpretation of this scene. The play's evocation of the events of chivalric romance sets up a species of dialogue between the on-stage action and the procedures of the traditional story, encouraging the spectator to ponder the workings of the one in the light of the other. The inherited tale, as noted above, is male-authored in that it is narrated from the hero's point of view, and the bride achieved in the course of his endeavours is assumed to be complicit in his goals. Shakespeare's alternative version of the tale of the chivalric quest interrogates the gender expectations implicit in this assumption. By reversing the terms of the traditional story and making the man the object of choice, he defamiliarizes the conventional situation, obliging the members of the audience to view a customary process with new eyes. The terms in which Bertram speaks are only marginally gender specific (in that he refers to a 'wife', and to a prospective partner as 'she') and it is useful to consider the implications that his lines would have held for a reader had they been spoken by the 'prize' of the conventional tale:

> Ber.   I shall beseech your highness,
>   In such a business give me leave to use
>   The help of mine own eyes.
> King.   Know'st thou not …
>   What she has done for me?
> Ber.   Yes, my good lord,
>   But never hope to knor why I should marry her.
>   …
>   I cannot love her nor will strive to do't.
>
> (II.iii.106–45)

In the mouth of a female character, the repudiation of patriarchal authority and resistance to a proposed marriage would define the speaker as a 'shrew' or 'scold', and thus as a disruptive force within the play world. By reversing the conventional tale, however, and making the man the object of choice, the dramatist turns the traditionally compliant reward for virtuous endeavour into a site of resistance to social norms, while evading the gender stereotyping that might otherwise ensue. In conceding the force of Bertram's objection to being given without consultation in marriage, the spectator is responding to a cry for human dignity that implicitly calls in question the role conventionally assigned to women, and thus encourages consideration of the female point of view. Where the damsel won by the valiant knight has no voice in the traditional tale, Helena's choice feels empowered by virtue of his sex to question the position in which he finds himself placed, unconsciously problematizing the very assumptions to which he appeals.

While Bertram's protest offers an insight into a conventionally female predicament, the uneasiness experienced by the spectator at the Count's situation (deriving in large measure from the fact that he is a man) invites a comparison between the capabilities of the sexes. The assumed inferiority that would warrant the conventional subjugation of women and justify the spectator's discomfort at Bertram's predicament is not borne out in the course of the action, which consistently elevates the female characters and exposes the limitations of the masculine world. The King's male physicians, for all their presumed skill (cf. I.iii.232–7), are unable to effect his cure; Bertram is disobedient, easily swayed and mendacious (cf. II.iii.261ff; II.iii.274–82; V.iii.80ff.); while Parolles is a garrulous coward, ready to betray his comrades to save his own life (cf. IV.iii.113ff.). The Countess, by contrast, is wise and generous (cf. her conduct towards Helena and her son); Helena is courageous and capable of self-sacrifice (cf. her plan to win the King, and readiness to abjure the world for her husband's sake, III.iv.4–17), while Diana and the Widow who aid Helena in Florence, are quick to come to another's aid (cf. IV.vii, *passim*). The 'masculine' virtues, in short, are here exhibited not by the male characters, but by the women whom Bertram attempts to position within their traditional roles, while it is the men who display the physical and mental deficiencies conventionally associated with the female sex. The uneasiness aroused in II.iii by the seemingly demeaning position in which the hero is placed is thus set in a wider context that serves to authenticate the Clown's recognition that a 'man [can] be at woman's command, and yet no hurt done' (I.iii.89–90).

Whereas the marriage between the knight and the damsel constitutes the climax of the conventional tale and the moment of joyful renewal in a cycle of death and rebirth, in Shakespeare's antithetical version of the story the heroine's election of her husband initiates a period of sterility and decay. While Boccaccio's Count merely 'sought the King's permission to depart [after his marriage] saying that he wished to return to his own estates and consummate his marriage there', [but instead] 'came to Tuscany, where he learned that the Florentines were waging war' (p. 308), Shakespeare's reluctant husband repeatedly stresses his refusal to share a bed with his bride (cf. 'I will not bed her', 'I'll to the Tuscan wars and never bed her', II.iii.266 and 269), and declines in an enactment of the non-consummation of their union to understand her request for a kiss:

> Hel. I am not worthy of the wealth I owe,
>   Nor dare I say 'tis mine – and yet it is;
>   But, like a timorous thief, most fain would steal
>   What law does vouch mine own.
> Ber.   What would you have?
> Hel. Something, and scarce so much; nothing indeed.
>   I would not tell you what I would, my lord.
>   Faith, yes:
>   Strangers and foes do sunder and not kiss.
> Ber. I pray you, stay not, but in haste to horse.

                                                    (II.v.79–87)

Rather than acceding to Helena's and the King's wishes, he resolves while still in Paris to throw himself into a conflict of no relevance to his own land, preferring the dangers of battle to his wife's bed (cf. 'I'll send her straight away. Tomorrow / I'll to the wars, she to her single sorrow', II.iii.291–2).

Helena's career subsequent to her repudiation by Bertram also bears witness to the sterility proceeding from the Count's decision. Just as the youthful husband leaves his native land for the Italian wars, where he turns to lust rather than sanctified love, so Helena leaves France on a pilgrimage, abjuring the world and thus all hope of fruition:

> I am Saint Jaques' pilgrim, thither gone.
> Ambitious love hath so in me offended
> That barefoot plod I the cold ground upon,
> With sainted vow my faults to have amended.
> …
> Bless him [Bertram] at home in peace, whilst I from far
> His name with zealous fervour sanctify.
> His taken labours bid him me forgive;
> I, his despiteful Juno, sent him forth
> From courtly friends, with camping foes to live

Where death and danger dogs the heels of worth.
He is too good and fair for death and me;
Whom I myself embrace to set him free.

(III.iv.4–17)

Though Helena's quest is finally achieved at the end of the play, and
a process of renewal is implied in that she is pregnant by her husband, it
is notable that the closing moments of the action again hold up a mirror
to the ending of the conventional story through a significant reshaping
of Boccaccio's tale. Whereas in the *Decameron*, Gilette prostrates herself
before her husband, having fulfilled his conditions for winning his
acceptance, and is raised by the Count who smothers her 'with kisses
and embraces' (p. 314), Helena retains her ascendancy over Bertram
throughout the closing scene, fulfilling her desires and holding out the
promise of a new order in both claiming and reclaiming the husband she
has won. Bertram's misconduct is at once recapitulated and augmented,
in that he denies his discreditable behaviour towards Diana, and it is
Helena who comes to his rescue, exculpating him of incontinency and
suspected murder. Rather than magnanimously accepting his wife,
Bertram is driven to recognize his own faults, and embraces the opportunity for social rehabilitation that his marriage offers in a spirit not of
joy but of relief. Once again, it is the women, rather than the men, who
function as the force of renewal in the world of the play, and the reit-
eration of the gnomic title in the King's closing lines ('All yet seems
well, and if it end so meet', V.iii.327) serves, like the Clown's comment, to justify the propriety of the denouement.

While *All's Well That Ends Well* may be regarded as a radical reworking
of that group of stories represented by Wilkins' tale of the shipwrecked
prince, Wilkins' narrative itself is indebted to another Shakespearian play.
Pericles, probably written some three or four years after the composition of
All's Well, is based upon Book 8 of John Gower's *Confessio Amantis*
(1393) and Laurence Twine's *The Patterne of Painefull Adventures* (c.1594),
and it is from the Shakespearian play, augmented with material derived
from Twine, that Wilkins' story, in turn, is constructed. Unlike *All's Well
That Ends Well*, *Pericles* is firmly located from the outset within the framework of romance, the action distanced from the audience by a mediaeval
narrator who is at pains to assert the antiquity of the tale he has come to
present:

To sing a song that old was sung,
From ashes ancient Gower is come,

Assuming man's infirmities,
To glad your ear, and please your eyes.
It hath been sung at festivals,
On ember-eves and holy-ales;
And lords and ladies in their lives
Have read it for restoratives:
The purchase is to make men glorious,
Et bonum quo antiquius eo melius.

(1 Chorus, 1–10)

The action follows the career of the title figure, who sets off to win a
bride by solving a riddle but discovers a dangerous secret and is obliged
to flee his land, losing his possessions, and falling victim to the elements,
but finally achieving a wife, a daughter and the approbation of the gods
through the exhibition of manly virtue. While the plot confirms the
dramatist's indebtedness to the chivalric romance, however, and itself
contributes through Wilkins' redaction, to the evolution of the tradition, the action simultaneously reveals Shakespeare's awareness of his
own earlier work in the process of composition. Having been shipwrecked and succoured by fishermen, Pericles presents himself at the
court of Simonides, taking part in a tournament, and winning the admiration through his gentility and prowess of the princess, Thaisa.
Aware of his daughter's feelings, Simonides confronts his impoverished
guest, seeking to force him to disclose his love of the youthful princess:

Sim. Let me ask you one thing:
    What do you think of my daughter, sir?
Per. A most virtuous princess.
Sim. And she is fair too, is she not?
Per. As a fair day in summer, wondrous fair.
Sim. Sir, my daughter thinks very well of you;
    Ay, so well, that you must be her master,
    And she will be your scholar: therefore look to it.
Per. I am unworthy for her schoolmaster.
Sim. She thinks not so; peruse this writing else.
    ...
Per. [*Kneels.*] O, seek not to entrap me, gracious lord,
    A stranger and distressed gentleman,
    That never aim'd so high to love your daughter,
    But bent all offices to honour her.
    ...
Sim. Here comes my daughter, she can witness it.
                        Enter Thaisa.

Per. Then, as you are as virtuous as fair,
  Resolve your angry father, if my tongue
  Did e'er solicit, or my hand subscribe
  To any syllable that made love to you.
Thai. Why, sir, say if you had, who takes offence
  At that would make me glad?
Sim. Yea, mistress, are you so peremptory?
  Aside. I am glad on't with all my heart. –
  I'll tame you, I'll bring you in subjection.
...
  Therefore hear you, mistress: either frame
  Your will to mine; and you, sir, hear you:
  Either be rul'd by me, or I'll make you –
  Man and wife.

                                        (II.v.32–83)

This scene clearly has much in common with the encounter between Helena and the Countess in *All's Well That Ends Well*, I.iii, and it is hard to believe that the dramatist was not conscious of the earlier play while composing the later scene. In both instances a seemingly possessive parent challenges a person of low condition with having fallen in love with their only child, inviting the members of the audience to anticipate an angry confrontation and the frustration of a suit. In the event, however, both parents violate audience expectation through the magnanimity of their behaviour, recognizing the virtue of the superficially unworthy lover and actively promoting the match. The similarity between the two scenes helps to confirm the dramatist's conception of *All's Well That Ends Well* as a version of the chivalric quest, while exhibiting the process of reversal at work in the construction of the play. In *Pericles* the angry parent is a father, the conventional head of the family group, while the superficially unworthy lover is in fact of noble blood, his true rank obscured by a series of misfortunes. The object of their debate is a virtuous princess, who has been quick to recognize her lowly suitor's worth, and whose wishes therefore coincide with those of her father. In *All's Well That Ends Well*, by contrast, the seemingly hostile parent is a maternal figure, while the unworthy suitor is a female dependent, whose only dowry is her inherent worth. The object of their debate, the Countess's son, is of dubious virtue, while his desires run counter to those of his mother in that he is reluctant to embrace her choice. Where *Pericles* looks backwards through its narrator to a legendary antiquity in which gender stereotypes hold good, *All's*

Well That Ends Well presents a less self-consciously fictive world, invert-ing romance conventions and thus subjecting the ideology encoded within them to fresh inspection.

It is this process of defamiliarization exemplified in the relationship between these two scenes that makes *All's Well That Ends Well* a key text for contemporary gender studies. At the heart of the twentieth-century feminist project is the exposure of the constructed nature of social institutions, and *All's Well That Ends Well* with its inversion of sexual norms is readily appropriated to this agenda. Where the 'purchase' of Gower's tale is 'to make *men* glorious' (1 Chorus, 9), the drive of *All's Well That Ends Well* is towards the achievement of a female 'project' (cf. 'My project may deceive me, / But my intents are fix'd, and will not leave me', I.i.224–5), giving the play a striking modernity. While *Pericles* and its narrative offshoot endorse the proposi-tion that '*Et bonum quo antiquius eo melius*'[15] (1 Chorus, 10), *All's Well That Ends Well* challenges the assumption that all old things are neces-sarily good.

15. 'And the older a good thing is, the better it is.'

Chapter 6

Cymbeline and the Tale of the Substitute Bedmate

The merchant's daughter, [it being dark and believing the stranger to be] her accustomed friend, used all courteous and most kind welcomes that might be, with wonderful protestations of her love, being such indeed as proceeded from deep-grounded affection, which made Parismus [the stranger] use the like courteous embracings, and thankful gratulations, finding by her speeches and by many other likelihoods that she was none of the basest, but might be of better parentage than he took her to be, which somewhat enticed his mind to a wandering delight in her kindness, that he determined with her to taste what love was. By that time they had continued their kindness a good space, she desired him to come by into her chamber, whither she led him in the dark, the poor soul having no other intent but chaste and virtuous, and nothing suspecting him to be a stranger, which Parismus well perceived by her behaviour. As soon as they were come thither, she kindly desired him to sit down on the bedside whilst she went to light a candle, as well to be delighted with beholding his person as otherwise.

She was no sooner gone, but Parismus secretly stepped to the door with purpose to behold if her beauty and person were agreeable to her other conditions, and saw her to be a most gallant and beautiful damsel, which sight so enticed his mind that as soon as she was coming to him with the candle he blew the same out, and told her that a light fitted not at that time, for it might be a means to betray their secret meeting, which she allowed for a sufficient excuse. Wherewith Parismus began to entertain her with such kind dalliance as erst she never tasted, kindly reproving his behaviour, yet had no power to resist. At which time (to both their delights) he deprived her of the jewel she was unwilling to lose, but with his pithy persuasions yielded unto, he using such a sweet attractive virtue as was able to conquer the chastest. Parismus reaped such sweet content from this virgin's pure delightful body that he was altogether unwilling to leave her pleasant embracings, but at last, remembering his estate, told her that he would work such means for safeguard of her honour as she should well like of. The poor soul with weeping eyes and hearty sighs bad him adieu.

(Emanuel Forde, *The Famous History of Parismus*, 1598)[1]

The tale of Parismus and Violetta is representative of a class of stories to which Shakespeare returned throughout his dramatic career. The plot, of considerable antiquity, and a frequent component of romance, turns upon the misidentification of a sexual partner, and lends itself to a variety of treatments, from the amusing to the potentially tragic. It appears first in Shakespearian drama in *The Comedy of Errors*[2] (1590–3) in a scene adapted from Plautus' *Menaechmi*, a play which itself looks back to a Greek original. A traveller, arriving in a strange city finds himself invited to dinner by a woman he has never met, and who insists upon the intimate nature of their relationship (cf. *Menaechmi* II.i, *The Comedy of Errors*, II.ii). In this instance the error arises from the fact that the newcomer has been mistaken for his identical twin, and numerous similar misunderstandings ensue before the brothers are brought face to face. Familial likeness is also the cause of the misadventures of the distressed heroines of drama and romance, whose experiences combine with those of the twins of *The Comedy of Errors* to create the confusions of *Twelfth Night* (1601). The story of Apolonius and Silla, for example, in Barnabe Riche's *Riche his Farewell to Militarie Profession* (1581) centres upon the adventures of a sister and her brother, the former disguised as a page following her shipwreck in a foreign land. The seeming youth is sent by the man she loves (and whose service she has entered) as his emissary to another woman, who in turn falls in love with her suitor's 'page'. The impasse thus created is resolved by the arrival of the heroine's brother, who is mistakenly welcomed into the house of his sister's female admirer, and promptly exploits the opportunity to make love to her. The story existed in numerous sixteenth-century versions,[3] with *Twelfth Night* representing the high point of its evolution. Once again a pair of twins is separated, the woman disguising herself as a man and thus attracting the affections of a member of her own sex. On

1. Based upon the version of the text in Geoffrey Bullough (1957–75), *Narrative and Dramatic Sources of Shakespeare*, vol.ii, Routledge and Kegan Paul, pp. 364–5. Spelling and punctuation, however, have been modernized. The passage quoted is from ch. XII.
2. This assumes the conventional dating of the corpus and that *The Comedy of Errors* precedes *Love's Labour's Lost*.
3. For a fuller discusssion of this complex of stories and their relationship with the Shakespearian corpus see Bullough, *Narrative and Dramatic Sources of Shakespeare*, vol. ii, pp. 269ff. and my (1992) *Shakespeare's Mouldy Tales*, Longman, pp. 24ff.

encountering the heroine's brother, the lady is deceived by the siblings' likeness, and thus unwittingly courts and marries a stranger. Whereas in romance versions of the story the encounter between the lady and the substitute lover is productive of shame or distress of mind, in *Twelfth Night* the marriage between Sebastian and Olivia achieves a sense of wondering assent through the singleness of identity of the two siblings:

> Duke. One face, one voice, one habit, and two persons!
>   A natural perspective, that is, and is not!
>   …
>
> Ant[onio]. How have you made division of yourself?
>   An apple cleft in two is not more twin
>   Than these two creatures. Which is Sebastian?
> Olivia. Most wonderful!
>   …
>
> Seb[astian]. So comes it, lady, you have been mistook.
>   But nature to her bias drew in that.
>   You would have been contracted to a maid;
>   Nor are you therein, by my life, deceiv'd:
>   You are betroth'd both to a maid and man.

(V.i.214–61)

As the tale of Parismus and Violetta indicates, however, the mis-identification of a sexual partner may arise from circumstances other than family resemblance. Darkness is a frequent motif in this complex of stories, and once again its use is exemplified in the Shakespearian corpus. In *The Merry Wives of Windsor* (1597), for example, a succession of suitors plan to elope with Anne Page at midnight in the darkness of the Great Park only to find that two of the prospective husbands have been tricked into 'marrying' boys. In this instance the motif is a comic one, emblematic of the more profound misalliance that Anne's marriage to either would represent, while contributing to the removal of obstacles to a more suitable union. The mistaken couplings are presumed by the audience to be unconsummated, and are productive of chagrin and social embarrassment rather than emotional confusion or guilt.

A far more complex range of emotions is triggered by that cluster of stories in which a substitution is engineered in the bedroom itself. In Boccaccio's tale of Gilette of Narbonne, for example (*Decameron*, Day 3, Story 9), the device constitutes the means by which the heroine escapes her predicament as a virgin bride and wins the admiration of her husband for her wit. The story represents an inversion of the tale of Parismus and Violetta in that in this instance the deception turns upon male rather than female credulity. Having been required to become pregnant by the man she has married, although he has firmly foresworn her bed, the heroine succeeds in fulfilling her seemingly impossible task by substituting herself in a darkened bedchamber for another woman whom her husband had sought to seduce. The story, retold in Painter's *The Palace of Pleasure*, is a principal source of *All's Well That Ends Well* (see above, Chapter 5, *passim*) where the action is set in a metaphorically darker arena. In this instance, although the heroine succeeds in fulfilling the task assigned to her by her husband and thus exhibits her worth as a wife, the nocturnal encounter in the bedroom has wider implications, probing the morality of the deception itself. Whereas Boccaccio focuses upon the adventures of the heroine, Shakespeare is equally concerned with the situation of the husband, and the impropriety of the actions in which he engages. His attempt to corrupt a virtuous woman is vividly presented in the course of the play, the substitution that takes place in the gloom of the bedchamber functioning not merely to achieve the heroine's objectives, but to salvage her partner's honour, while permitting him to experience the shame and guilt of his intents. The moral loading of the story is thus much greater in *All's Well That Ends Well* than in the sources from which it derives, inviting the audience to reflect upon the ethics of a situation 'where both not sin, and yet a sinful fact' (III.vii.47).[4]

It is *Measure for Measure* (1604), however, which presents the most disturbing version of the substitute bedmate story (prior to Shakespeare's inversion of the tale in *Cymbeline*), while exhibiting the richness of its potential for the exploration of moral issues. Where Forde's *Parismus* is merely an adventurer and his Violetta a trusting young woman, Shakespeare's central figures in this play are the embodiments of extreme positions, Angelo (the Duke's deputy) seeking to uphold an ideal of justice, and Isabella (a prospective nun) a life of chastity. A meeting between the two in which Isabella petitions for the life of her brother, condemned to death for fornication, serves to fire the lust of the deputy, prompting him into an attempt to blackmail her into exchanging her virginity for her brother's release. The sexual encounter that he seeks to instigate is thus based on coercion rather than upon consent, the depth of corruption that it signifies signalled by the violent terms in which he formulates the proposal:

---

4. For a fuller discussion of Shakespeare's treatment of the bed trick in this play (and *Measure for Measure*) see my *Shakespeare's Mouldy Tales*, pp. 100ff.

I have begun,
And now I give my sensual race the rein:
Fit thy consent to my sharp appetite;
Lay by all nicety and prolixious blushes
That banish what they sue for. Redeem thy brother
By yielding up thy body to my will;
Or else he must not only die the death,
But thy unkindness shall his death draw out
To ling'ring sufferance.

(II.iv.158–66)

As in *All's Well That Ends Well*, however, the dishonourable intentions of the would-be seducer are subverted by the provision of an alternative sexual partner. Mariana, formerly betrothed to Angelo, is substituted by the Duke for Isabella, becoming the deputy's wife at the moment of their union.[5] Theoretically, the encounter is thus a morally acceptable one, but it remains, nevertheless, highly disturbing both for the dramatis personae and those outside the play world. Although in embracing 'Isabella' Angelo is in fact consummating his marriage, he believes himself to be violating a woman who has dedicated herself to God, subjecting Mariana to an act of rape, rather than an expression of love. Mariana herself is receiving the embraces intended for another woman, while Isabella in promoting the encounter is saving her honour by engaging in deceit. The incident is thus a richly ambivalent one, allowing for the resolution of the situation and thus the achievement of a comic ending, while drawing the audience into the world of tragic experience, where lives and even souls are in jeopardy, and moral issues are far from clear cut.

The potential of the tale of the substitute bedmate for the exploration of the darkest human impulses within a comic framework makes the story a peculiarly appropriate one for the final phase of Shakespeare's work. The plays of the dramatist's last period are crowded with 'hypothetical' situations in which the dramatis personae confront as realities events which prove to be fictitious. Leontes, in *The Winter's Tale* (1610–11), for example, repents for sixteen years of being the cause of his wife's death, only to have her restored to him in the final scene, while Alonso in *The Tempest*, having accepted the loss of his only son as

5. For a full discussion of the law of precontract and its application to *Measure for Measure* see Ernest Schanzer, 'The Marriage-Contracts in *Measure for Measure*', *Shakespeare Survey* 13, Cambridge University Press (1960), pp. 81–9.

a fitting punishment for his sins, is reunited with him at the close of the play. For all its appropriateness to the fictive experiences of the dramatist's romances, however, the presence of the motif of the substitute partner within this group of plays is not readily detected. Rather than simply transposing the device from *Measure for Measure* to *Cymbeline*, (the final play in which it occurs), Shakespeare constructs a far more elusive version of his inherited story, alluding to it and weaving variations upon it, before permitting it finally to surface towards the close of the play in its most intellectual challenging mutation.

Whereas in *The Comedy of Errors* Adriana's mistake in accepting a total stranger as her husband is carefully prepared for from the outset of the play by the emphasis placed by the dramatist upon the identical nature of the two men (cf. the errors of identification that take place in I.ii. and II.ii.), in *Cymbeline* it is upon the contrast between Cloten and Posthumus, one of whom is ultimately to be mistaken for the other, upon which the attention of the audience is focused. The play opens with a conversation between two unnamed gentlemen, whose function is to supply the audience with background information before the entrance of the central figures, and a large part of their dialogue is devoted to the contrast between the princess's suitors:

> First Gent. You do not meet a man but frowns: our bloods
>   No more obey the heavens than our courtiers
>   Still seem as does the king's.
> Sec. Gent.   But what's the matter?
> First Gent. His daughter, and the sole heir of's kingdom (whom
>   He purpos'd to his wife's sole son – a widow
>   That late he married) hath referr'd herself
>   Unto a poor but worthy gentleman. She's wedded,
>   Her husband banish'd; she imprison'd, all
>   Is outward sorrow, though I think the king
>   Be touch'd at very heart.
> Sec. Gent.   None but the king?
> First Gent. He that hath lost her too: so is the queen,
>   That most desir'd the match. But not a courtier,
>   Although they wear their faces to the bent
>   Of the king's looks, hath a heart that is not
>   Glad at the thing they scowl at.
> Sec. Gent.   And why so?
> First Gent. He that hath miss'd the princess is a thing
>   Too bad for bad report: and he that hath her
>   (I mean, that married her, alack good man,

And therefore banish'd) is a creature such
As, to seek through the regions of the earth
For one his like; there would be something failing
In him that should compare. I do not think
So fair an outward, and such stuff within
Endows a man, but he.
    ...
Sec. Gent. What's his name and birth?
First Gent. I cannot delve him to the root: his father
Was call'd Sicilius ...
And had (besides this gentleman in question)
Two other sons, who in the wars o'th'time
Died with their swords in hand. For which their father,
Then old, and fond of issue, took such sorrow
That he quit being; and his gentle lady,
Big of this gentleman (our theme) deceas'd
As he was born. The king he takes the babe
To his protection, calls him Posthumus Leonatus,
Breeds him, and makes him of his bed-chamber,
Puts to him all the learnings that his time
Could make him the receiver of.

(I.i.1–44)

A systematic opposition is clearly set up here between the two com-
petitors for the princess's hand. Cloten (as yet unnamed) is the queen's
son by her first marriage, and thus the step-brother of the woman
(Imogen) he wishes to marry, while Posthumus is the king's protégé, and
thus her father's ward. Cloten is a comparative newcomer to the court as
the King has only 'lately' married his mother, whereas Posthumus was
bred there and was close to the king from his earliest years. Cloten's
arrival as Cymbeline's stepson is closely followed by Posthumus' banishment on becoming the king's son-in-law, while the rise of the former's
worldly fortunes is balanced against the other's achievement of the
princess's love. More significantly, the two men are also diametrically
opposed in moral terms. Whereas Cloten is incomparably vicious (cf.
'too bad for bad report'), Posthumus is a paragon of virtue, 'a creature
such / As, to seek through the regions of the earth / For one his like;
there would be something failing / In him that should compare'.

The confrontation between Imogen and her father in the following
scene sustains the contrastive process set up in the opening lines.
Cymbeline repudiates Posthumus as 'thou basest thing' (I.ii.56),
rejecting him for his 'unworthiness' (I.ii.58) and it is upon the relative

value of her two suitors that the princess's exchange with her father centres. Where Cymbeline stresses the lack of worldly fortune that makes Posthumus an inappropriate choice for the heir to the throne, Imogen is emphatic that it is qualities of mind rather than wealth or station that determine human worth:

> Cym.   O disloyal thing,
> ...
>   That mightst have had the sole son of my queen!
> Imo. O blessed, that I might not! I chose an eagle,
>   And did avoid a puttock.
> Cym. Thou took'st a beggar, wouldst have made my throne
>   A seat for baseness.
> Imo.   No, I rather added
>   A lustre to it.
> Cym.   O thou vile one!
> Imo.   Sir,
>   It is your fault that I have lov'd Posthumus:
>   You bred him as my playfellow, and he is
>   A man worth any woman: overbuys me
>   Almost the sum he pays.
>
> (I.ii.62–78)

The entrance of Cloten himself in the following scene simultaneously confirms the validity of the princess's stance here, while sustaining the polarization between her two suitors established by earlier speakers. The First Gentleman's celebration of the moral and intellectual gifts that have made Posthumus an ideal courtier is in sharp contrast to the image of the queen's son that is projected in I.iii. The First Gentleman notes Posthumus' receptivity to the education that he received through Cymbeline's patronage, and the model that he offered to other members of the court, cf:

> [The king]
> Puts to him [Posthumus] all the learnings that his time
> Could make him the receiver of, which he took,
> As we do air, fast as 'twas minister'd,
> And in's spring became a harvest: liv'd in court
> (Which rare it is to do) most prais'd, most lov'd;
> A sample to the youngest, to th'more mature
> A glass that feated them, and to the graver
> A child that guided dotards.
>
> (I.i.43–50)

Cloten's deficiencies as a courtier, by contrast, are immediately apparent. The opening lines of I.iii. emphasize that he is physically unappealing, in that he smells overpoweringly after taking part in a fencing bout, while the opening exchanges establish that he has no expertise in a discipline conventionally included among the gentlemanly arts (cf. 'Clo. Have I hurt him?' / Sec Lord. [*Aside*] 'No faith: not so much as his patience', I.ii.5–6). The attitudes of the two courtiers attending him, moreover, exhibit his more serious failings as a prince. Rather than seeking to model his conduct upon him, the First Lord flatters him to the point of absurdity in the hope of gaining his favour, while the Second despises his folly, insistently deriding him in asides, cf:

> Clo. The villain would not stand me.
> Sec. Lord. [*Aside*] No, but he fled forward still, toward
>   your face.
> First Lord. Stand you? You have land enough of your
>   own: but he added to your having, gave you some
>   ground.
> Sec. Lord. [*Aside*] As many inches as you have oceans.
>   Puppies!
> Clo. I would they had not come between us.
> Sec. Lord. [*Aside*] So would I, till you had measur'd how
>   long a fool you were upon the ground.

(I.ii.13–23)

His second appearance, in II.i, moreover, heightens the impression of physical and mental degeneracy conveyed in previous scenes. Once again he enters lamenting his lack of success in a contest, betraying, as he regrets the loss of his wager, his incapacity for courtly life and incomprehension of the obligations of rank:

> Clo. Was there ever man had such luck? When I kissed
>   the jack upon an upcast, to be hit away! I had a
>   hundred pound on't: and then a whoreson jackanapes
>   must take me up for swearing, as if I borrowed mine
>   oaths of him, and might not spend them at my pleasure.
> First Lord. What got he by that? You have broke his pate
>   with your bowl.
> Sec. Lord. [*Aside*] If his wit had been like him that broke
>   it, it would have run all out.
> Clo. When a gentleman is dispos'd to swear, it is not for
>   any standers-by to curtail his oaths. Ha?
> Sec. Lord. No, my lord; [*Aside*] nor crop the ears of them.

> Clo. Whoreson dog! I gave him satisfaction! Would he
>   had been one of my rank!
> Sec. Lord. [*Aside*] To have smelt like a fool ...
>   It is not fit your lordship should undertake
>   every companion that you give offence to.
> Clo. No, I know that: but it is fit I should commit offence
>   to my inferiors.

(II.i.1–29)

A third entrance, in II.iii, reiterates the same points, while once again stressing, through what is to prove a significant image, the opposite pole that he embodies from Posthumus, whom he still hopes to supplant in Imogen's bed. Yet again he makes his appearance discussing his ill success at a game, with the implication that he has once more lost a wager (cf. II.iii.1–8). The courtship of Imogen that he then attempts is initiated with a lewd comment to the musicians whom he has employed to aid his suit, his ribaldry serving as an index to the degeneracy of his mind, while he reveals his depth of hatred and lack of understanding of his rival in a manner that prompts an emphatic response:

> Clo. The contract you pretend with that base wretch,
>   One bred of alms, and foster'd with cold dishes,
>   With scraps o'th'court, it is no contract, none;
>   And though it be allow'd in meaner parties
>   (Yet who than he more mean?) to knit their souls
>   (On whom there is no more dependency
>   But brats and beggary) in self-figur'd knot,
>   Yet you are curb'd from that enlargement, by
>   The consequence o' th' crown, and must not foil
>   The precious note of it; with a base slave,
>   A hilding or a livery, a squire's cloth,
>   A pantler; not so eminent.
> Imo.   Profane fellow,
>   Wert thou the son of Jupiter, and no more
>   But what thou art besides, thou wert too base
>   To be his groom.
>   ...
> Clo.   The south-fog rot him!
> Imo. He never can meet more mischance than come
>   To be but nam'd of thee. His mean'st garment,
>   That ever hath but clipp'd his body, is dearer
>   In my respect, than all the hairs above thee,
>   Were they all made such men.

(II.iii.112–35)

Once again, the extremes of two kinds of baseness, social and moral, are opposed here, with Posthumus embodying the former in the eyes of Cloten, and Cloten representing for Imogen the epitome of the latter. The princess's assertion that she cares more for her husband's meanest garment than for a host of men such as Cloten serves, however, to initiate a process that is to bring the two men into greater proximity. Infuriated by the insult, to which he constantly returns (cf. II.iii.138, 149, 155), Cloten plans to obtain a suit of his rival's garments and to revenge himself upon the woman who has rejected him by ravishing her while dressed in Posthumus' clothes:

> Clo. She said upon a time (the bitterness
> of it I now belch from my heart) that she
> held the very garment of Posthumus in more respect
> than my noble and natural person; together with
> the adornment of my qualities. With that suit upon
> my back, will I ravish her: first kill him, and in her
> eyes; there shall she see my valour, which will then
> be a torment to her contempt. He on the ground,
> my speech of insultment ended on his dead body,
> and when my lust hath dined (which, as I say, to
> vex her I will execute in the clothes that she so
> prais'd) to the court I'll knock her back.
>
> (III.v.134–45)

In scheming to kill his rival and rape his wife while dressed in his garments Cloten is not merely planning a peculiarly perverse revenge (reminiscent of the rape of Lavinia in *Titus Andronicus*), he is proposing to engage in a species of substitution. By dressing in the other man's clothes, he becomes physically more like him, more susceptible of the kind of mistaking that drives the plot of *The Comedy of Errors*. At the same time, moreover, that Cloten plans to move closer to his alter ego in terms of physical appearance, Posthumus embarks on a process that is to bring his moral character into a much greater degree of alignment with that of his reputed reverse. Having travelled to Italy after his banishment from Britain, he engages in a wager (cf. Cloten's succession of wagers noted above), gambling on Imogen's chastity, and thus facilitating a dishonourable attempt on his wife's virtue. Once convinced (erroneously) that he has lost the contest (cf. Cloten's ill-success in a series of games), he resorts like his seeming opposite to violence, contemplating tearing his wife to pieces in the presence of her father, while exhibiting both a lewd imagination and a misogynistic impulse in his reflections upon the female sex:

> Post. O, that I had her here, to tear her limb-meal!
> I will go there and do't, i'th' court, before
> Her father.
> ...
> This yellow Iachimo, in an hour, was't not?
> Or less; at first? Perchance he spoke not, but
> Like a full-acorn'd boar, a German one,
> Cried 'O!' and mounted; found no opposition
> But what he look'd for should oppose and she
> Should from encounter guard. Could I find out
> The woman's part in me – for there's no motion
> That tends to vice in man, but I affirm
> It is the woman's part: be it lying, note it,
> The woman's: flattering, hers; deceiving, hers:
> Lust, and rank thoughts, hers, hers: revenges, hers:
> Ambitions, covetings, change of prides, disdain,
> Nice longings, slanders, mutability;
> All faults that name, nay, that hell knows, why, hers
> In part, or all.

(II.iv.147–80)

The catalogue of vices that Posthumus lists here could well apply to himself, indicating how far he has fallen from the man described in the opening scene. Just as Cloten plans to kill him, he in turn orders Imogen's death, bringing his mind, as his servant remarks, into line with his fortunes (cf. III.ii.10–11). The gulf that initially existed between the princess's suitors is thus closed in both physical and moral terms, while the correspondences set up between them invite the audience to perceive them as twinned.

While the relationship between Posthumus and Cloten represents a variation upon the motif of the identical sibling, the situations in which Imogen is placed or envisaged make up a thread of allusions to the theme of the substitute sexual partner. In I.vii, for example, Iachimo seeks to convince Imogen that Posthumus has been unfaithful to her, and proposes that she revenge herself on her husband by admitting him (i.e. Iachimo) to her bed (cf. Cloten's plan to revenge himself on Posthumus by Imogen's rape). Iachimo having retracted his proposal as a device to try her virtue, Imogen accepts his 'trunk' for safekeeping in her bedchamber (anticipating the different 'trunk' she is to lie with in

IV.ii.), and thus unknowingly admits into her bedroom the man committed to her dishonour. The scene in which her custodianship of the trunk is proposed is full of sexual innuendo, encouraging those outside the play world to anticipate the probable intentions of her would-be seducer:

> Iach. I am something curious, being strange,
>   To have them [his 'jewels'] in safe stowage: may it please you
>   To take them in protection?
> Imo.   Willingly:
>   And pawn mine honour for their safety, since
>   My lord hath interest in them; I will keep them
>   In my bedchamber.
> Iach.   They are in a trunk
>   Attended by my men: I will make bold
>   To send them to you, only for this night.
>   ...
> Imo. Send your trunk to me, it shall be safely kept,
>   And truly yielded you.
>
>   (I.vii.191–210)

The nocturnal scene which follows their agreement heightens the apprehensions of the audience, while embracing a range of sexual allusions. The scene opens upon Imogen's bedchamber dominated by her bed and the ominous trunk, while the opening exchanges emphasize the lateness of the hour and the single taper lighting the room. The book Imogen is reading before she lies down to sleep is the story of Philomel, and she breaks off at the moment of the heroine's rape (cf. II.ii.44–6). Before giving way to sleep, she prays to be protected from 'tempters of the night' (II.ii.9), and is defenceless when Iachimo emerges from the trunk.[6] The Italian compares himself to Tarquin as he approaches her, inviting the supposition that he is intent upon rape, while he subjects her body to a scrutiny appropriate only to a husband or a lover. In slipping off her bracelet, a gift from Posthumus, he symbolically deflowers her, enjoying an intimacy with her of which she is unaware and which runs counter to her intentions. The scene is reenacted, moreover, in Iachimo's report of it to Posthumus during which further details of the bedchamber are supplied. Once again, the images evoked are highly erotic, serving to associate the heroine in the imaginations of the

---

6. For a most perceptive step-by-step analysis of the development of this scene see Brian Gibbons (1993) *Shakespeare and Multiplicity*, Cambridge University Press, pp. 42ff. to which I am indebted at a number of points.

listeners (both inside and outside the play world) with a range of sexual encounters:

> Iach.   First, her bedchamber,
> (Where I confess I slept not, but profess
> Had that was well worth watching) it was hang'd
> With tapestry of silk and silver, the story
> Proud Cleopatra, when she met her Roman,
> And Cydnus swell'd above the banks, or for
> The press of boats or pride.
> ...
>   The chimney
> Is south the chamber, and the chimney-piece,
> Chaste Dian, bathing: never saw I figures
> So likely to report themselves; the cutter
> Was as another Nature, dumb; outwent her,
> Motion and breath left out.
> ...
>   The roof o'th'chamber
> With golden cherubins is fretted. Her andirons
> (I had forgot them) were two winking Cupids
> Of silver, each on one foot standing, nicely
> Depending on their brands.
>
> (II.iv.66–91)

What is achieved by Iachimo in the course of this description is a kaleidoscopic version of an alternative Imogen, at the opposite pole from the chaste princess who angrily repelled his suit. The description of the hangings of her bedchamber serves to associate her with the most highly erotic of Egyptian queens, who embraced a succession of lovers, while Iachimo's lengthy account of the beauty of her statuette (cf. lines 81–4) implies his voyeuristic enjoyment of its owner. The presence of Cupids suggests a place dedicated not to chastity but the rites of love, while the crossed feet of the andirons indicates sleep, and thus the consummation of love. The speaker's detailed knowledge of the bedchamber insinuates a similar intimacy with its occupant, inviting the spectator to imagine him as another Antony, or as one of the sleeping lovers lit by the 'brands' of the 'winking Cupids'.

Iachimo's evocation of a sensual Imogen ready to receive him in her husband's place is quickly supplanted by Posthumus' version of his wife as a greedily unselective, and hence animalistic, wanton (cf. II.iv.165–71, see page 142). Once again, the audience is presented with an imagined encounter between the heroine and a substitute sexual partner, with the elegant Italian, Iachimo, now transformed, in the fevered imagination of the man he has sought to deceive, into a German boar. The transmutations Imogen undergoes in the minds of the male figures combine to endow her, for those outside the play world, with a range of hypothetical existences other than her perceived roles as princess and wife and this excursion into fictive experience is complicated when Imogen herself elects to assume the part of a boy. Informed that her husband has planned to kill her, she is encouraged by Pisanio to pose as a youth and thus to adopt male rather than female characteristics:

> Pis. You must forget to be a woman: change
>   Command into obedience: fear, and niceness
>   (The handmaids of all women, or, more truly,
>   Woman it pretty self) into a waggish courage,
>   Ready in gibes, quick-answer'd, saucy, and
>   As quarrelous as the weasel: nay, you must
>   Forget that rarest treasure of your cheek,
>   Exposing it (but, O, the harder heart!
>   Alack, no remedy) to the greedy touch
>   Of common-kissing Titan: and forget
>   Your laboursome and dainty trims, wherein
>   You made great Juno angry.[7]

(III.iv.156–67)

Throughout the remainder of the action Imogen is dressed as a youth, and it is as a boy that she is received by those she subsequently encounters. Having travelled to Wales, experiencing the hardships of life as a man (cf. III.vi. *passim*), she enters upon a life yet further removed from that of Cymbeline's daughter in becoming cave-keeper to a group of mountain dwellers. Numerous strands of fiction are drawn together at this point, in that all the characters involved are literally or figuratively disguised, and all are in some way deceived by a false appearance. Imogen herself has assumed the role of a boy, while the youths whom she encounters are not in reality mountain men, but her brothers stolen in infancy from the court. Sick as a consequence of her journey, she takes a potion which induces a profound sleep, but which her hosts, finding her lifeless, mistake for death. The 'mountaineers' then perform a funeral service over the seemingly dead 'youth', consigning 'him' sadly

---

7. A further substitute partner for Imogen (Jove, notoriously susceptible to human beauty) is implied here through Juno's anger at the heroine's 'dainty trims'.

to the earth. The complexities of this scene do not end, however, at this point. Cloten, himself dressed in the garments of Posthumus, is misled by the appearance of the elder of the two rustics, and misguidedly attempts to kill him. Slain by the man who is in fact his step-brother, he is decapitated and his headless body is then laid out beside that of the supposedly dead youth. The fiction that Cloten devised has thus become a reality, in that he does indeed lie with Imogen while dressed in her husband's clothes. The nuptial bed he sought to share with her, however, has become a death bed, while the flowers with which their faces are strewn mark, not the completion of the marriage he once hoped for, but the consignment of their bodies to the earth.

It is at the moment of Imogen's waking, however, that the many strands of the substitute bedmate motif are finally drawn together in a highly complex inversion of the conventional tale. Awakening from her drugged sleep, Imogen is at first uncertain where she is, believing that she is still on the long journey to Milford Haven, that she has travelled all night, and is on the verge of sleep. Growing more aware of her surroundings, she becomes conscious of the body beside her, recognizes the garments, and instantly identifies the dead man in the most positive terms as her husband:

> Imo. [*Awakes*] Yes sir, to Milford-Haven, which is the way?
> I thank you: by yond bush? pray, how far thither?
> 'Ods pittikins: can it be six mile yet?
> I have gone all night: faith I'll lie down and sleep.
> But, soft! no bedfellow! O gods and goddesses!
> > [*Seeing the body of Cloten.*
> These flowers are like the pleasures of the world;
> This bloody man, the care on't. I hope I dream:
> For so I thought I was a cave-keeper,
> And cook to honest creatures. But 'tis not so:
> 'Twas but a bolt of nothing, shot at nothing,
> Which the brain makes of fumes. Our very eyes
> Are sometimes like our judgements, blind. Good faith,
> I tremble still with fear: but if there be
> Yet left in heaven as small a drop of pity
> As a wren's eye, fear'd gods, a part of it!
> The dream's here still: even when I wake it is
> Without me, as within me: not imagin'd, felt.
> A headless man? The garments of Posthumus?
> I know the shape of's leg: this is his hand:
> His foot Mercurial: his Martial thigh:

The brawns of Hercules: but his Jovial face –
Murder in heaven! How – ? 'Tis gone. Pisanio,
All curses madded Hecuba gave the Greeks,
And mine to boot, be darted on thee! Thou,
Conspir'd with that irregulous devil, Cloten,
Hast here cut off my lord. To write, and read
Be henceforth treacherous! Damn'd Pisanio
Hath with his forged letters (damn'd Pisanio)
From this most bravest vessel of the world
Struck the main-top! O Posthumus, alas,
Where is thy head? where's that? Ay me! where's that?
Pisanio might have kill'd thee at the heart,
And left this head on. How should this be, Pisanio?
'Tis he, and Cloten: malice and lucre in them
Have laid this woe here. O, 'tis pregnant, pregnant!
The drug he gave me, which he said was precious
And cordial to me, have I not found it
Murd'rous to th'senses? That confirms it home:
This is Pisanio's deed, and Cloten – O!
Give colour to my pale cheek with thy blood,
That we the horrider may seem to those
Which chance to find us. O, my lord! my lord!
                              [*Falls on the body.*
                                              (IV.ii.291–332)

All the elements of the traditional tale of the substitute bedmate are invoked in the course of this speech. Imogen's opening lines suggest a nocturnal encounter, the lady is deceived by the interchangeability of her suitors, and embraces a strange 'bedfellow' in the conviction that he is her chosen partner. In fact, however, the circumstances in which the deception takes place represent a reversal of those of the inherited story. Although Imogen has been sleeping, she wakens into daylight, not darkness, and makes her false identification, unlike Bertram in *All's Well That Ends Well* or Angelo in *Measure for Measure*, on the basis of what she sees. At the same time, it is the contrast rather than the likeness (as in *The Comedy of Errors* or *Twelfth Night*) that has been stressed between her suitors, yet Imogen is nevertheless quick to 'recognize' the man beside her as her husband for all her earlier emphasis on the distance between them. Moreover, whereas in the traditional story it is the alternative suitor who exploits an unexpected opportunity (cf. *The History of Parismus*), here it is the lady who is the active agent in the encounter, with the substitute partner passive beneath her exploring hands. The head that is lost and lamented is not the maidenhead that defines a woman's sexual status, but the cranium that distinguishes man from man (cf. the similar play upon 'head' and 'maidenhead' discussed in Chapter 4 above), while the blood of the ruptured hymen is here the life blood of the supposed loved one, smeared in grief on the heroine's face.

The responses produced by this scene in the course of performance are curiously mixed. On the one hand, the grief that Imogen exhibits is profoundly moving, while on the other her confident misidentification of the body, her exclamations over the missing head, and constant references to Cloten are both ludicrous and highly ironic. The wit involved in the inversion of the conventional story itself has a distancing effect, while the knowledge that Imogen is wrong, and that Posthumus is alive, permits those outside the play world to reflect upon the implications of the action rather than viewing the situation exclusively from the heroine's point of view. The ease with which Imogen mistakes her husband for his opposite invites reflection upon the nature of human identity, while providing support for her own proposition that 'Our very eyes / Are sometimes like our judgements, blind'.[8]

While lending itself, however, through the mixed signals that it generates, to the procedures of conventional criticism with its traditional preoccupations with the treatment of character, audience alignment, levels of artifice and theme, Imogen's misidentification of Cloten is susceptible to analysis in terms of a very different methodology. In scrutinizing the form of the man she believes to be her husband, she is engaged in attempting to read the text of his body, to decipher its meaning by virtue of signs with which she is familiar, and she is thus involved in an exercise analogous to that of a reader confronted with words on a printed page. It is her deductions in the course of this activity which makes this scene a peculiarly interesting one for the modern reader. Structuralism, the critical revolution that lies at the heart of mid to late twentieth-century literary discourse, is fundamentally concerned with the sign system that is language, and the means by which the informed reader decodes, or makes sense of, a text. For the structuralist critic, the 'signifier' (in the case of the written language, the mark on the printed page), and the 'signifed' (the concept to which the signifier refers) are the two halves of a single coin that constitute the 'sign' (i.e. the written or spoken word), meaning being communicated from one

8. For a fuller discussion of the complex nature of this scene, see my (1988) *Discovering Shakespeare's Meaning*, Macmillan, 2nd edn, Longman, 1994), pp. 194ff.

person to another, not because the sign relates directly to a world of preconceived ideas, but because the reader or listener recognizes a system of rules and relationships that govern, and hence make sense of, the text. The point may be illustrated by reference to the road signs (many of which now transcend national and linguistic barriers) which govern the movement of traffic. Single and double yellow lines have no logical connection with parking restrictions, yet their meaning is understood by drivers who distinguish between the significance of the two. The stable relationship between the two halves of the sign (signified and signified) has been challenged, however, by poststructuralist criticism and it is in this context that Imogen's reading of the text of Cloten's body may be seen as contributing to a twentieth-century debate. Recent criticism has exhibited the protean nature of the signified, and the importance of context in signification.[9] In the same way that an artefact may carry a religious significance in one culture, while capable of being viewed or read in purely aesthetic terms by those from a different social group,[10] so other kinds of signifier may gather new meanings according to context, or the framework within which they are located.

The moment of Imogen's awakening provides a striking instance of the instability of the relationship between signifier and signified. Imogen assumes the inexorable unity of the sign and thus is led to the conclusion that the dead body beside her is that of her husband. For the members of the audience, by contrast, the inferences drawn by the heroine constitute a significant misreading of the text. The marks upon which she focuses (e.g. 'the shape of's leg') carry a different significance for those outside the play world, exhibiting the range of meanings that a body of material may yield for different readers. At the same time, Imogen is engaged not merely in decoding a set of signifiers, but in the construction of a narrative. Having 'recognized' the body as that of Posthumus, she proceeds to deduce the process that has brought about her husband's death, casting Cloten as the instigator of his murder, and Pisanio as her step-brother's instrument (cf. IV.ii.312–16). The drug that Pisanio gave her, formerly an index of his kindness (cf. III.iv.189–95), is now read as evidence of his guilt (cf. IV.ii.325–9), while the two men are supplied with motives on the basis of their former actions, and in the case of Pisanio his limited means (cf.

---

9. For the elusive nature of the signified see in particular the work of Roland Barthes.
10. I am indebted for this illustration to Raman Selden (1985, 2nd ed, 1989), *A Reader's Guide to Contemporary Literary Theory*, Harvester Wheatsheaf.

IV.ii.324–5). Imogen's story of the trunk is thus very different from that which has been followed by the audience, with the heroine constructing a tragic version of her own narrative at a considerable distance from the comic process in which for the audience she remains engaged.

Imogen's alternative reading of the tale of her substitute bedmate, while exhibiting the instability of the relationship between signifier and signified, also contributes to a deferment of meaning which is characteristic of the drama as a whole, and which again lends itself to analysis in poststructuralist critical terms. Rather than arriving at a truth, or an ultimate meaning, through her reading of the body, Imogen regresses into a fiction within the fiction of the play itself, and this movement is evident at other moments in the drama. Iachimo's account to Posthumus in II.iv, for example, of his visit to Imogen's bedchamber is a careful record of the details of a room, but once again the shifting relationship between the two halves of the sign leads to the generation of a new set of meanings in the context of a particular understanding. For Posthumus the hangings and ornaments noted by the Italian inscribe a particular cast of mind, while the bracelet that once registered the bond between the lovers becomes a token of infidelity. Presented with Iachimo's narrative of Imogen's bedchamber, Posthumus interrogates its meaning, constructing the tale of his wife's infidelity, and thus (like Imogen's story of Posthumus) a text within a text:

> Iach.   Will you hear more?
> Post. Spare your arithmetic, never count the turns:
>   Once, and a million!
> Iach.   I'll be sworn –
> Post.   No swearing:
>   If you will swear you have not done't you lie,
>   And I will kill thee if thou dost deny
>   Thou'st made me cuckold.
>   …
>   In an hour, was't not?
>   Or less; at first? Perchance he spoke not, but
>   Like a full-acorn'd boar, a German one,
>   Cried 'O!' and mounted.
>
> (II.iv.142–69)

Here, the story of a faithful wife whose chastity is unsuccessfully assailed by an embodiment of decadent sophistication becomes the tale of a rampant woman who embraces an animalistic suitor at the first approach.

The discovery by a Roman captain (Lucius) of the prostrate Imogen embracing the dead partner who for the heroine is her lost husband and for the audience the unworthy Cloten, exhibits the same process of deferment and the consequent generation of multiple narratives. The spectacle, which constitutes for those outside the play world a variation on the tale of the substitute bedmate, is here reinterpreted becoming a story of a noble man and his page:

> Luc. Soft ho, what trunk is here?
> Without his top? The ruin speaks that sometime
> It was a worthy building. How? a page?
> Or dead, or sleeping on him? But dead rather:
> For nature doth abhor to make his bed
> With the defunct, or sleep upon the dead.
> Let's see the boy's face.
> Cap. He's alive, my lord.
> Luc. He'll then instruct us of this body. Young one,
> Inform us of thy fortunes, for it seems
> They crave to be demanded. Who is this
> Thou mak'st thy bloody pillow? Or who was he
> That (otherwise than noble Nature did)
> Hath alter'd that good picture? What's thy interest
> In this sad wreck? How came't? Who is't?
> What art thou?
> Imo. I am nothing; or if not,
> Nothing to be were better. This was my master,
> A very valiant Briton, and a good,
> That here by mountaineers lies slain.
> …
> Luc. Thy name?
> Imo. Fidele, sir.
> Luc. Thou dost approve thyself the very same:
> Thy name well fits thy faith; thy faith thy name:
> Wilt take thy chance with me? I will not say
> Thou shalt be so well master'd, but be sure
> No less belov'd.

> (IV.ii.353–84)

Like Imogen before him, Lucius here interrogates a set of signifiers deducing a meaning from them at variance both with the heroine's reading of her situation and the perceptions of those outside the play world. For the Roman, the prostrate forms are those of a boy and his master, the former a worthy individual (cf. lines 355 and 365), and the latter patently dead (lines 356–8). Once assured that the 'page' is in fact living, Lucius assumes that 'he' both can and will 'instruct' them about the history of the body, posing a series of questions that hold different answers for the spectator and the seeming youth to whom they are addressed. Rather than 'instructing' her listeners, however, Imogen further misinforms them, consciously constructing a new version of her own history and relationship with the dead man. Cloten's body, having been misread as that of Posthumus and then as that of a worthy gentleman, now becomes that of a valiant Briton, slain and beheaded by 'mountaineers'. Ironically, however, two of the details of Imogen's story coincide with the process witnessed by the theatre audience, in that the dead man was British and slain by a supposed rustic, lending authenticity to the third element of her story, that the body is that of a worthy man. Cloten thus enjoys a 'posthumus' existence in this scene in more than one sense. Not only is he dressed in his rival's clothes and mistaken for him by the princess, he is accepted by Lucius as a heroic figure, while his reinvention brings him closer to his alter ego for those outside the play world. An ignoble figure in one narrative is thus the hero of another, challenging the concept of stable identity advanced in the play's opening lines while contributing to a proliferation of tales.

Lucius' interrogation of the 'boy' himself (as opposed to the situation of his dead 'master') also serves to plunge the audience into a process that moves progressively further from any firm actuality or ultimate truth. Lucius enquires 'his' name and is informed that it is 'Fidele', the response serving to confirm the masculine identity of the speaker and thus extending the fiction on which Imogen embarked on first assuming her disguise. The 'meaning', however, of 'Fidele' has shifted from its significance in earlier scenes. For the mountaineers the term signified the youth who looked after their cave and whom they regarded as a brother, while for Lucius it is the name of a page faithful to his master unto death. The Roman's response, 'Thou dost approve thyself the very same', is thus a more complex observation for the theatre audience than it is for the speaker, while his decision to take the boy into his service functions once again to authenticate an initial misreading of the text. For Lucius the dead man was a kind and loving master whom he intends to emulate in his behaviour towards his page, thus transforming Imogen's fictive version of her history into an actuality, while the heroine herself is incorporated into her own re-reading of the text in entering the Roman's service.

Imogen's initial response on being asked to identify herself ('I am nothing', IV.ii.367), while summing up her sense of the meaninglessness of a life without her husband, may also be seen as expressing the progressive dissolution of stable identity that has been effected in the course of the play. First understood by the audience as a British princess who has married beneath her station, she undergoes a series of mutations in a multiplication of narratives that serve to fragment her personality both for the spectator and those within the play world. Having begun the play as a newly married woman, the object of her father's anger and Cloten's aspirations, she becomes a whore in the eyes of her husband, 'dies' to the members of her society, assumes a masculine identity, regresses into a superficially more primitive environment, 'dies' again and returns to life as a widow, and awakens from a paroxysm of grief to a fresh existence as a page. Rather than isolating the universally agreed characteristics of a unique individual, the signifier 'Imogen' thus initiates a seemingly endless chain of signifieds – undutiful daughter, loving wife, chaste woman, whore, boy, brother, cook, widow, servant. At the same time, Imogen's own deductions about her situation constitute a narrative that does not correspond with any larger framework, or the stories in which others believe themselves to be located. Lucius' version of his meeting with 'Fidele' does not coincide with Imogen's own, while neither accords with that of the theatre audience, and the same is true of Posthumus' story of his relationship with his wife. In short, the process of interpretation and construction of narrative in which the dramatis personae as a whole are engaged functions to dissolve the coherence not only of the individual but the universe in which the characters function, creating a condition of ontological uncertainty highly relevant to the postmodern world.

While the very different readings of the tale of the substitute bedmate offered by the dramatis personae in the course of *Cymbeline* lend themselves to interpretation in terms of twentieth-century critical and philosophical preoccupations, they also provide a model of the dramatist's own methodology, and it is for this reason that the discussion of Shakespeare's treatment of his borrowed plot in this play has been reserved for the conclusion of the present study. Just as his characters construct alternative versions of the texts with which they are presented, weaving new, autonomous fictions through their own idiosyncratic interrogation of the data before them, so Shakespeare is engaged throughout his dramatic career not merely in the recapitulation of others' material, but in the fabrication of fresh narratives from the stories on which he draws, and the realization of new potentialities through the perspectives from which he inspects them. Posthumus, framing the story of his wife's infidelity, or Imogen elaborating the tale of her husband's death, may thus be seen as engaging in a kind of activity comparable with that of their own creator reading the history of Parismus and Violetta.

Just as his characters' generation of multiple narratives is analagous to his own procedures, moreover, so the process in which Shakespeare himself is engaged in his approach to his source material is comparable with that of the twentieth-century critic in relation to canonical literary texts. The assumption that creative works carry unequivocal meanings that are the product of an author's intention and remain constant from generation to generation has given way (as noted above) in the modern period to the concept of the text as unstable, its meaning dictated in large measure by the context in which it is situated and the preoccupations of its reader. Just as Shakespeare constructs alternative stories from the narratives with which he is engaged, so the modern critic has constructed 'alternative Shakespeares'[11] through the different methodologies applied to the dramatist's work, fragmenting the body of critical discourse. The ideal receptive consciousness has given place to a multiplicity of readers, each with his or her own narrative of the text, disassociating it from any fixed intention on the part of its creator, and thus rendering its future significance impossible to predict.

The implications of this development for all those engaged on any level with the business of wrestling with words are clearly far-reaching and are enunciated, fittingly, by Imogen as she seeks to interrogate the text of her 'husband's' body. Intended as a curse, but susceptible, perhaps, of re-reading as a benediction, her words could well stand as a motto for all late twentieth-century literary activity –

'To write, and read / Be henceforth treacherous'.

11. The phrase forms the title of a collection of essays edited by John Drakakis (Methuen, 1985)

Further Reading

The cornerstone of the study of Shakespeare's source material remains Geoffrey Bullough's monumental (1957–75) *Narrative and Dramatic Sources of Shakespeare* (8 vols), Routledge and Kegan Paul. The study not only draws together the major sources and analogues of the Shakespearian corpus and thus constitutes a treasure house of 'tales' in its own right, it also explores the dramatist's treatment of his inherited material and provides substantial bibliographies of both secondary studies and primary texts.

The material presented by Bullough may be placed in a larger context by reference to the major collections of stories to which Shakespeare turned either directly or through intermediaries throughout his dramatic career, notably Giovanni Boccaccio (written 1349–51) *The Decameron*, now available as a Penguin Classic, ed. G.H. McWilliam (1972); and William Painter (1556, 1567 and 1575) *The Palace of Pleasure*, most recently edited in four volumes by Hamish Miles (1929), Cresset Press. Modern collections of Elizabethan stories are also helpful in contextualizing the motifs explored in the plays. The third section of Kenneth Muir (ed.) (1956), *Elizabethan and Jacobean Prose*, Penguin, offers a broad selection of Renaissance tales and dramatic situations, while T.J.B. Spenser (ed.) (1968) *Elizabethan Love Stories*, Penguin, draws together eight love stories adapted by Shakespeare and briefly discusses their history. The introductions to the more scholarly modern editions of the plays (e.g. Arden, New Cambridge, Signet) also provide extracts from source material for comparison with the plays, and consider the adaptations made by the dramatist in the course of composition.

The secondary literature concerned with the playwright's use of earlier material adopts a variety of approaches to the subject and thus offers a number of different routes by which to engage with this aspect of Shakespeare studies. K. Muir (1978), *The Sources of Shakespeare's Plays*, Yale University Press, for example, is concerned with the broad spectrum of the corpus, and the handling of source material in plays of different genres, whereas M.M. Lascelles (1953) *Shakespeare's 'Measure for Measure'*, The Athlone Press, and C.T.Prouty (1950), *The Sources of 'Much Ado About Nothing'*, Yale University Press, focus upon particular items in the canon, exploring their antecedents in considerable depth. My own (1992) *Shakespeare's Mouldy Tales*, Longman, by contrast, is primarily concerned, not with the pre-history of Shakespeare's borrowed material but with the process of adaptation that it undergoes in the course of his work, tracing the dramatist's re-use of particular plot motifs in a succession of plays, and locating his approach to his source materials in the context of Renaissance concepts of the creative process. Of relevance also here is that type of study concerned with Shakespeare's reading and thus the intellectual background against which his work took shape. Among this group, G.K. Hunter, 'Shakespeare's Reading', in K. Muir and S. Schoenbaum (eds) (1971) *A New Companion to Shakespeare Studies*, Cambridge University Press, pp.55–66 is particularly helpful and has a useful bibliography (p. 265).

The new approaches to literary studies that have emerged in recent years have given rise to a huge volume of publications, many of which may appear abstruse and difficult of access at first approach. The concluding chapter (by Jonathan Dollimore) of Stanley Wells (ed.) (1990) *Shakespeare: A Bibliographical Guide*, Clarendon Press, (pp. 405–28), offers a starting point for the study of these developments, discussing the impact of Cultural Materialism, Gender Criticism and New Historicism on current attitudes to the Shakespearian corpus. A more detailed, yet admirably lucid, introduction to the range of late twentieth-century critical thought is afforded by Raman Selden (1985, 2nd edn, 1989) *A Reader's Guide to Contemporary Literary Theory*, Harvester Wheatsheaf, which explores all the critical methodologies touched on in the course of this book, while providing full bibliographies of the trends discussed. A number of genre-based collections of essays provide a first step towards the understanding of the application of the new approaches to specific areas of the Shakespearian corpus. Particularly useful here are Garry Waller (ed.) (1991) *Shakespeare's Comedies*, Longman; John Drakakis (ed.) (1992) *Shakespearean Tragedy*, Longman; and Graham Holderness (ed.) (1992) *Shakespeare's History Plays: 'Richard II' to 'Henry V'*, Macmillan, all of which offer accounts of the plays in terms of late twentieth-century critical developments, and include suggestions for further reading.

Any selection of volumes devoted to specific literary approaches must necessarily be arbitrary, but the following have either established themselves as of particular importance in their own right or bring together a range of significant material: Stephen Greenblatt (1988) *Shakespearean Negotiations: The Circulation of Social Energy in Renaissance England*, Oxford University Press, (New Historicism); C.R.S. Lenz, G. Greene and C.T. Neely (1980) *The Woman's Part: Feminist Criticism of Shakespeare*, University of Illinois Press, (Feminist Studies); Jonathan Dollimore and Alan Sinfield (eds) (1985) *Political Shakespeare*, Manchester University Press, (Cultural Materialism); Terence Hawkes (1977) *Structuralism and Semiotics*, Methuen, (Structuralism); Malcolm Evans (1986) *Signifying Nothing: Truth's True Contents in Shakespeare's Text*, Harvester Press, (Deconstruction).

Finally, mention must be made of John Drakakis (ed.) (1985) *Alternative Shakespeares*, Methuen, a stimulating collection of fresh approaches to the corpus which, in conjunction with Geoffrey Bullough's, *Narrative and Dramatic Sources of Shakespeare*, might be said to have provided the point of departure for this book.

Index